Tripod Finds a Friend And Other Stories

Stories of Wildlife Rescue and Rehabilitation

Dr. ROOPA SATISH with ANITHA MURTHY

To my parents Prema and Satish and my sister Deepa, who were with me from the beginning of my journey in wildlife field, encouraging and supporting me through all the ups and downs.

Roopa

Contents

Preface

Bannerghatta Rehabilitation Centre is a unique wildlife hospital set up inside Bannerghatta forest by an NGO – Wildlife Rescue and Rehabilitation Centre (WRRC) – along with the Karnataka Forest Department. It was established in 2000 and depends on voluntary donations from individuals, companies, and institutions for funding.

Since its opening, we have rescued and rehabilitated more than 20,000 wild animals belonging to more than nine species of mammals, thirty-five species of birds, and eleven species of reptiles.

In the fourteen years that I have worked in rehabilitation, every case has been special, but they cannot all be included here for obvious reasons. The cases that were selected for inclusion in this book were the ones that stayed in my mind and were imprinted on my heart because of the indomitable spirit, strong will, and never-say-die attitude of the wild animals. Hope you enjoy reading their stories.

Dr. Roopa Satish, May 2023

1. TRIPOD FINDS A FRIEND

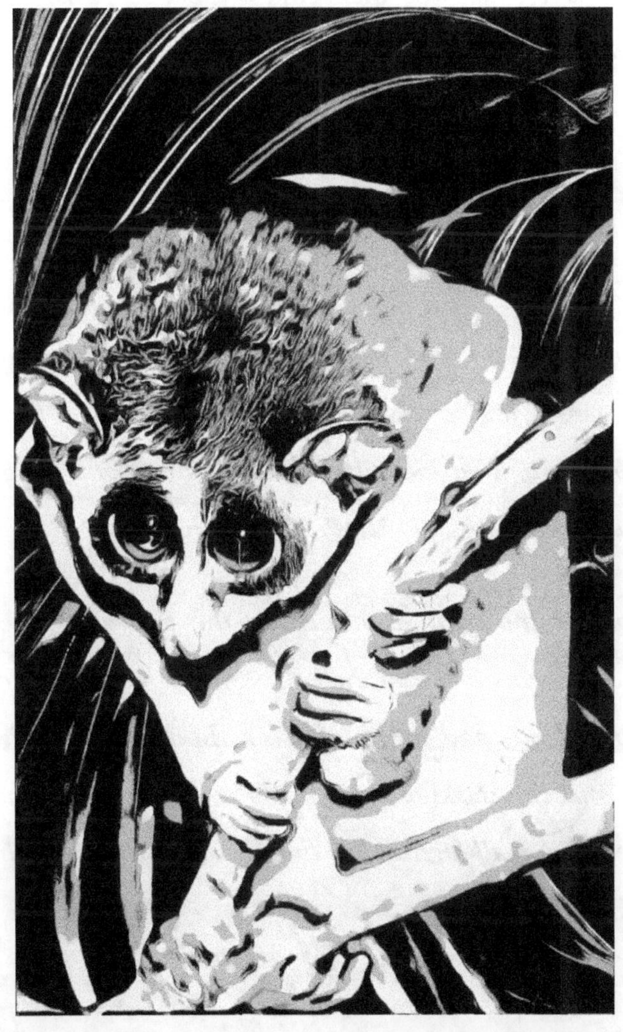

Slender Loris (*Loris lydekkerianus*)

A version of this story was first published online by "Animal Poetics" theme of the Teesta Review (May 2022).

The waning moon hangs like a silver bow in the dark sky. The thick canopy of the trees absorbs the inky blackness of the still night like a sponge. There is no breeze, which makes the rustling sound more ominous. Two shadows make their way cautiously in silence.

"Look. Up there." One figure nudges the other, as they peer into the darkness.

One of them reaches for his torch and switches it on. The beam swings across the leaves, searching till it bounces off something that looks like a pair of headlights gleaming in the darkness. Mission accomplished.

One of the men shimmies up the tree and plucks a round furball off the branch. He drops the furball into a cardboard box and it lands with a thud. The two figures melt into the darkness gripping the box tightly. They've made their small fortune for the night. It's as easy as that.

There's a nip in the air on a September morning when I reach my office. It isn't an office in the usual sense, the kind that is coming up all over Bangalore. The city is abuzz with construction activity: roads and flyovers and underpasses are springing up any which way you turn, high-rise apartment complexes are rapidly extending into the areas around the city proper, and glass seems to be the in thing to build with, never mind that it is not at all suitable to the climate of the place and will consume energy like a monster because of the air-conditioning required. Bangalore is a happening city, people from all over the country, and indeed the world, are flocking to it, and no one cares about how all the development is stripping the land of its natural resources.

I am glad that the centre I work at is far away from the city. It is part of the Bannerghatta Biological Park. Just one acre of the allotted seven acres houses the buildings – the rest is left untouched, with its trees and plants and animals. It is a haven indeed, where I can breathe in clean air and believe that living in harmony with nature is possible. I have always loved animals, and have studied to become a vet. And now I work with rescuing and rehabilitating wild animals.

There's nothing that gives me more happiness than to see untampered wildlife, existing as nature meant it to be.

As I settle into my chair and begin to look at some paperwork, I hear the noise of a vehicle approaching the centre and wonder who that could be. Curious, I walk out to the entrance, joined by my boys. An auto stops in front of the building, and I recognize the rescuer who emerges; he is one of the many working with our centre. BBMP (Bruhat Bengaluru Mahanagara Palike), which is the

governing authority for the city, has its own helpline that people can call if they spot a wild animal in distress, or if they need any assistance with say, snakes or monkeys on their premises. Apart from those employed by the BBMP, there are several volunteer rescuers, who do this kind of work as a service out of love for animals. But there are others too, who do this for a fee. Everyone has their own motivation, I guess. But what's important is that these rescuers play a vital role in getting animals out of places where they are not welcome to a more appropriate environment.

"Good morning," I call out. "You've brought something for me?"

"Good morning, ma'am," He smiles, lifting a carboard box out of the auto. My boys help him to bring it into the centre.

"It is a slender loris, ma'am," he tells me. "It is in bad shape. It was found lying on the road."

"A slender loris?" I am intrigued.

Slender loris is a really shy and small primate found in Southern India and Sri Lanka. In Kannada, it is called Kaadu paapa, or jungle baby. It has these large saucer shaped eyes that make it look quite adorable. People in Bangalore are not even aware that they share their city with this unique and tiny mammal. Slender lorises are solitary creatures though many may live on the same tree. Places like the Indian Institute of Science and surrounding areas which have a continuous canopy cover are ideal for these animals to make homes there. It is wonderful that there are still pockets of this city which are green and provide a good habitat for such wildlife.

We take the box into the "consulting room". The box has airholes poked into it for ventilation after taping it shut. Most animals when rescued come to us like this. The rescuers often have little or no equipment so an appropriately sized carboard carton from a nearby kirana shop will be used to house the creature for transport.

We first weigh the box along with the slender loris inside it. My rule of thumb is to treat the animal based on its exact body weight. We cannot always draw blood samples or do scans on the animals. Sometimes they are too tiny and sometimes they are just too weak to tolerate such tests. So, I base my medication doses on the body weight. Instead of stressing the animal out by lifting it out of the box and trying to position it on the scales, I just weigh the entire box. Later, I can subtract the weight of the empty box from this weight to get the exact weight of the animal.

Once I've noted this down, it's time to open the box. We need to be really careful now.

Just imagine you were happily playing with your friends, and suddenly, you were dragged away, hurt badly, and left on the road. If anyone tried to come near you and help, you would be very suspicious and careful, wouldn't you? And if you felt you were in the slightest danger, wouldn't you want to run away or turn around and attack?

Rescued wild animals pretty much feel the same way. They are unpredictable in their behaviour. Since they are almost always rescued from unnatural surroundings, they are already stressed out completely, and they could easily lash out by biting or attacking.

But my boys are well-trained. They know how to handle all kinds of animals, and without them, I would never be able to treat the animals. I trust my boys with my life! We also communicate by just signs and signals, because we want to make the least amount of noise. Unexpected and loud noises will upset the animal even more, and we definitely don't want that.

The boys make sure that the eyes of the loris are covered with a cloth when they lift it out of the box. They also know exactly how to hold it. They grip its neck through a cloth. This way, both vision and tactile information to the animal is reduced, and so the stress to the loris is reduced as well.

Once the boys have the loris in position, I examine it thoroughly. I need to check for temperature, swelling or inflammation or redness anywhere, or loss of function. Now it is really very difficult to figure out if a slender loris is a male or a female because their identifying parts are hidden! So, for purposes of this narration, let's assume the loris that has been rescued is a female.

As I examine her, my heart goes out to her. She is absolutely traumatized and petrified by whatever has happened. I inspect her carefully, and as I see the burn wounds on her hands and legs, and precise cuts made on the palm, forearm and arm of her left forelimb, I feel a surge of anger. These are definitely not injuries that have occurred in the wild because of say, another animal attacking or a fight with another loris. No, these burn wounds and precise cuts point to one and only one thing: human involvement.

India is a wonderful land of ancient culture and heritage, and we should indeed feel proud of it. But what of the terrible superstitions that still run deep? You might be surprised to know, but there are many, many people who still believe in things like black magic. Babas and fake gurus often take advantage of people's fears and make them believe that things like enchanted nimboos or sacrificial chicken or goats will help them get what they want, or make their enemies suffer. Unfortunately, the slender loris is also a tool used in black magic rituals. Since they are nocturnal animals, they are hunted during the night. The slender loris is harmless and has no defence mechanism as such. No claws that scratch or sharp teeth that bite. Its cousin – the slow loris – at least has a venomous bite.

However, the slender loris does not, and so falls prey to people who want to capture it for black magic. They use the slender loris as a voodoo doll, so whatever injury they inflict on it, they believe their enemy will suffer the same way.

I shudder as I remember a heart-breaking incident earlier, where a slender loris that was brought in showed no signs of injury on the outside, yet passed away quickly. An autopsy showed that its heart had been pricked and it had bled to death on the inside. I pray that this loris has not been attacked in the same way.

The left forelimb is in really bad shape and I am not sure if it will heal at all. It is already showing signs of necrosis, or rotting. I give her a pain-killer – that will definitely help in many ways.

It is now time to move her to a different place. Over the next few days, we do everything to take care of her.

We arrange for a sky kennel, which is basically a large solid plastic box with metal bars. We place the slender loris gently into the sky kennel and cover it with a cloth so that the daylight doesn't stress her out. I check out her diet and since she is insectivorous, I make sure that she has a daily diet of insects like cockroaches, dragonflies, and grasshoppers. We actually catch these critters in and around the centre. We also give her banana, which she really seems to like. The typical weight of a slender loris is 275 gms, but this one weighed only 165 gms when she was brought in. She really needs to eat up!

Every day I check on her, and every time I see her, I wonder how humans can be so cruel to animals. This slender loris looks like a sweet extra-terrestrial creature, somewhat like ET, with its large saucer-shaped eyes, slender body, and long gangly hands and legs. It is completely harmless, yet we seek it out and actively harm it.

She seems to be becoming a little better, but the left forelimb is a goner. There is no way to rescue it, and so, after a month of waiting and watching, we finally bring her in for surgery and amputate the left forelimb. The loris seems to recover more quickly after this. The amputation wound heals completely in a month, and we can even see her hair start to grow back on the stump. What a trooper she is!

Now that she's showing signs of becoming more active, we need to get her out of the sky kennel. We move her into a larger enclosure. Lined with coconut thatch to minimize the light, it has ample place to move around and hang about, and I am delighted to see that she is comfortable on just three limbs.

"She looks like a tripod," I laugh, and the name sticks. The boys, who clean and feed her and interact with her daily begin to call her Tripod. I normally do not name my animals. It makes me uncomfortable because once we name them, we begin to view them as pets. But these are not pets – they are wild animals, and should remain wild.

However, I cannot help it with Tripod. She is an exception – and a remarkable one at that. She is so shy, yet so curious and alert, always watching us with her large eyes as we clean her enclosure or give her food. She is so agile despite her amputated limb. She is a born survivor. It is hard indeed not to grow fond of her.

A few months later, the police bring in another loris, who appears to be yet another victim of the horrible black magic. This loris too has similar burn wounds, but is not in as bad a shape. I go through the same protocol of treatment. Once she has recovered in the sky kennel, we decide to introduce her to Tripod.

Now the slender loris as such is a solitary animal, and they go about foraging for food alone. However, they roost together in groups. Groups usually consist of not more than seven members, made up of a female and her offspring, and one or more males. They are nocturnal animals so they spend the entire day sleeping and are awake and about at night. Many of us are like the slender loris, aren't we? This is why they have such large eyes, which enable them to capture as much light as possible in the night in order to see.

We are quite curious about how Tripod will react to the new entrant. Slender lorises can communicate to each other through a variety of vocalisations, including whistles and chitters. Will Tripod welcome her new pal? Or will she be hostile and show signs of aggression?

We house Tripod and the new loris in adjacent enclosures, and watch carefully. They appear to be inquisitive about each other, and lose no time in communicating through the wire mesh that separates them. This is happy news indeed!

We move them both into the same enclosure, and as the days go by, we can see a discernible change in Tripod. She looks healthier and happier, and it looks like the two lorises are not just getting along fine, but actually helping each other heal, both physically and emotionally. They seem to have bonded very well, and are now acting like BFFs!

About three months later, we decide that it is time to release Tripod and her friend back into the wild. She is showing remarkable agility and adapting to her new three-legged life with ease. Her good friend is also supportive and together, we feel they can survive the wild very well. They really need the wider canopy of trees to feel at home, forage for food, and be themselves.

The release process is not straightforward; there are forms to be filled and permissions to be taken. But when all that is done, the day finally arrives.

These lorises feel like my babies and though I feel sad to let them go, I know that this is what is best for them. Wild animals should never be reduced to pets, meant to amuse and entertain and divert us humans. They deserve their own lives as nature made them and this is what I am meant to do.

We place the lorises in baskets with twigs that they can hold on to. Night is fast approaching when we travel to the designated release site in a safe, protected forest area. We carefully remove the twigs from the basket, with the lorises hanging on to them. We place these twigs strategically on the branches of a tree and step back.

Tripod and her friend look around hesitantly, and as we hold our breath, they cautiously let go of the twig and move to the branch. Feeling their way along the bark with their limbs, they climb up the tree and soon they have disappeared into its thick foliage.

We wait for a few minutes more before departing. Our job here is done. Tripod and her friend are back where they belong.

It's been several years now. Sometimes, I think of Tripod and wonder what she is up to. Was she able to survive the wild with the support of her friend? Is she still clambering up trees on her three legs and hunting for food? Has she started a family?

Wherever she is, I wish Tripod and her friend the best life they can have.

About the animal

- Slender Loris (Loris lydekkerianus) also called Gray Slender Loris, is native to South India and Sri Lanka.

- It is nocturnal (meaning active at night) and arboreal (meaning living in trees).

- It is insectivorous (meaning it eats insects), but it can also eat some veggie stuff.

- It has opposable thumbs, just like humans, so it can actually grip things.

- Fun-fact: it smears its entire body with its urine to protect itself against the stings and bites of the little insects it feeds on.

- It is a mammal, and gives birth to its young ones. Twins are common, and the males also help in child-care.

Why is it in danger?

- The Slender Loris is one of the animals protected under the Indian Wildlife Act of 1972, under Schedule 1, which includes highly endangered animals like the tigers.

- It cannot defend itself very well and falls easy prey to hunters.

- It is captured and used as a pet or as a source of captive entertainment.

- It is subjected to cruel treatment by practitioners of black magic.

- Its habitat of tree canopy is fast vanishing with unrestricted development.

2. MONKEY BUSINESS

Bonnet macaque (*Macaca radiata*)

The little monkey pauses and looks around. He is alone, separated from his troop while foraging, but he is a big boy, isn't he? He can manage quite well. After all, there have been so many things that he has learnt over the past five years. For instance, that grey ribbon that looks like a river? It isn't a river at all. It's called a road, it's made of hard stones, and strange things go whoosh! on it. He has to be careful of those strange things, because if he is unlucky enough to be caught by one, he is sure to die. The only way he can get across this stone river is to swing along these wires that are suspended overhead, almost as if inviting him to dangle from them.

So here he goes, swinging along, nice and easy, using three of his limbs to stay in contact with the wire at a time to reduce his swaying. What goes on in his mind as he crosses the road on this artificial trapeze? Is he thinking of the big tree canopy on the other side? Or is he missing his troop that is waiting for him?

Suddenly, there is a loud crackling sound. What is that? He looks around grimacing in fear, but before he knows it, there is a burning smell in the air, and he is falling...falling...falling...

I can barely recognize the creature I am staring down at.

"What happened?" I ask the locals who have brought it in.

"We saw this monkey falling to the ground," one of the men explains. "It was swinging from the electric wires, trying to get across the road. Suddenly, we heard a sizzling sound and saw it fall. We ran to rescue it, and put it into a cardboard box and brought it here. They said it will be taken care of in this place."

"Will it be okay?" Another man asks, looking rather anxious. "I think it suffered a rather big shock. Will it even live?"

I really don't know how to answer his question. This is supposed to be a Bonnet Macaque, a species of monkey specific to Southern India. Right now, it looks like a piece of burned meat. The smell is awful too.

"I'll see what I can do," I say, trying to use a reassuring voice while ushering the men out of the room. The little one is lucky that the men were around, and took prompt action. Other monkeys are not so fortunate sometimes.

When they finally leave, I head back to the injured primate. My heart is heavy, for I fear it might not be able to make it after all. The shock it has suffered is a real nasty one. The extremities are looking red. I need to cool the body down as soon as possible to stop it getting further cooked. Only then I can start any treatment. We hold him under running tap water to cool down the tissues and to stop further tissue damage. When muscles which are subjected to high voltage current, the tissues get cooked by the heat, literally converting muscle to meat. This is usually an irreversible process, and the areas which are badly burnt in the accident will now slowly rot (undergo necrosis), turn black, and finally will fall off. This could take from one week to a month.

Widespread urbanization is a curse for these wild animals. Their habitat gets completely destroyed and they are left with no place to go. Bonnet macaques live in a limited area in Southern India, and that area is being torn apart gradually. Development is happening all over the country, so now, bonnet macaques also have to compete with their counterparts from North India – the rhesus macaques – who are looking for fresh pastures, having been driven out from their original environment.

Bonnet macaques need widespread tree canopies to freely move from point to point by swinging on the branches. Cut the trees, and the monkeys have to look for alternate ways to survive. They end up using the electric transmission wires for locomotion and then suffer the terrible consequences like this poor monkey.

After the initial emergency treatment done to handle the pain, we put the little macaque under observation for necrosis. Three limbs – both forelimbs and the left hind limb – begin to show signs of rotting. It is certain that they will need to be amputated. Amputation surgery is undertaken only after it is clear which limbs are no longer viable, as well as how much of the limb has necrosed. This ensures that the blood loss during surgery is minimal, giving maximum chance of recovery. In this case, we wait for almost one and half months after the accident before we schedule his surgery.

Once the little one is ready for the operation, I get working with my boys to move the monkey to what is called the squeeze cage. There are different types of squeeze cages which are specifically built for treating animals. On this cage, there is a lever on the side, and when the lever is pressed, the bars of the cage slide closer and closer till the animal snugly fits, and it cannot twist or turn or move around. This is very important, since there cannot be sudden jerks or movements when we are treating the animals.

I sedate my little friend and when he has passed out, we move him into surgery. The affected limbs have now become all black and shrivelled. They are basically dead meat, and if left untended, they will rot, so I will be amputating them.

Once the surgery is all done, we wait for the sedation to wear off.

I am worried for he has now just one hind limb. How will the little guy manage? There is absolutely no question of releasing him back to the wild, for he will never be able to survive with practically no limbs. I know the loss of his family is a heavy price he has to pay, for bonnet macaques are very social animals, and being a troop member is an integral part of their lives. But there is little I can do, and I can only hope that he will recover and be as healthy as he can get. If all goes well and he survives this major operation, we can provide lifetime care at our centre. Not the ideal situation for a wild animal, whose true habitat is the jungle, but this is the best we can do.

When my friend recovers – and he does make a remarkable recovery – he begins to show his true colours.

Two weeks post-surgery, all the stumps of his limbs are healed very well. It is time for the next stage – he needs to be shifted into a bigger enclosure. This is a space specially prepared for him, and it has platforms and staircases for moving up and down and around. It is filled with foliage and branches, mud and earth, and it definitely has more room to move around than the squeeze cage he has been confined to for the past two months.

We watch the little macaque explore his new space hesitantly, and we wonder if he will be able to move at all, if not with his earlier agility.

His initial moves are tentative, but as the days pass by, he proves to be a complete surprise package. He works around his missing limbs so smartly, and uses his forelimb, chest, and tail to move around, swinging around with a carefree abandon. He has come such a long way from the burned blob that was carried into the centre! I am blown away by his resilience, and how superbly he has adapted to living with just one limb. It cannot be easy, but that does not stop him from swinging and hopping around, doing his own monkey things.

He is docile and friendly, and so we introduce some pet monkeys into his enclosure for company. He becomes, by default, the alpha of this motley group of macaques. What proves really fascinating is the effect he has on the pet monkeys

Now people love to own animals. Never mind if the animals are wild and never supposed to be domesticated. Take monkeys, for example. So many people think that having a pet monkey is a cool thing. They adore petting and cuddling them, and teach them "cute" tricks like begging for their food. But when monkeys hit puberty, they become aggressive. They bite and attack, and people who earlier worshipped them, get scared and dump them.

We have many such pet monkeys at our centre, who have unfortunately learned not to run the other way when confronted with human beings. A wild monkey will always make a dash away from a person, not the other way around. Pet monkeys however, will hang around, either to beg for food or to attack with or without any provocation.

Pet monkeys actually need to unlearn this behaviour. There is also a danger when several such monkeys are dumped into an enclosure together. Monkeys in the wild have a strict hierarchy. The dominant, or alpha monkey, has various ways of showing that he is the dominant member of the troop. The other submissive, or beta monkeys, have their own ways of showing that they submit to the dominant one. This kind of behaviour is crucial to the survival of the monkeys in the wild, for the hierarchy makes sure that every member of the troop knows his or her place. Pet monkeys unfortunately have no clue about this way of life, and have to be taught this behaviour if there is any chance of them being released back into the wilderness.

This is where our new macaque inmate comes in. He plays teacher to the pet monkeys, and guides them to revert to their true natural behaviour. Sometimes, with the different vocalizations that bonnet macaques are wont to make, it looks like he is almost chiding them about their unnatural habits, like demanding affection from the humans! He is indeed such an excellent teacher, and I am thrilled.

But our macaque is inquisitive, and is not content to be in captivity. He befriends our resident patriarch macaque Taatha, who is free to roam around in the centre. Taatha himself has been with us for the past sixteen years after he was rescued from a research

laboratory. The bonnet macaque interacts and communicates through the mesh with Taatha, and soon forms a deep bond with him.

So, it comes as no surprise to us when one fine day, when the boys come in to clean his enclosure, our little friend slips out. Very soon, he is spotted all over the tree canopy of the centre, following Taatha around.

He hops about, his gait reminding me so much of a kangaroo, that I laugh and begin to refer to him by that name.

"What is a kangaaroo, Akka?" One of my boys asks me, rather puzzled.

My boys are tribal boys, and know the forest and its creatures like the back of their hand. They have intimate knowledge of the living environment in the forest, they are brilliant at the local names of the animals and their behaviours, and they are masters at handling the creatures. But they have only a rather sparse knowledge of animals in other continents, so I show them pictures and videos of kangaroos on the web.

"Yes, you are right!" They laugh and agree. "Our monkey looks like a kangaaroo only!"

And thus, our little bonnet macaque gets christened. To an outsider, it must be quite baffling and amusing to have a monkey called Kangaroo, but to us, it seems to be rather appropriate.

It has been a little over two years now, and Kangaaroo has well and truly settled into life at the centre. We try to ensure that he hasn't become all tame and still retains his wild flavour. He doesn't hang around too much with us. He does show up sometimes in the evenings, requesting for a banana or two, but otherwise, he is pretty content to hang out by himself. He still is aware that humans are trouble in general, and makes sure to avoid any inquisitive visitors.

His recovery is nothing short of a miracle. His adaptation to the loss of limbs is remarkable. Even hair has regrown on the stumps of the limbs, and that is a true sign of healing.

There are so many lessons to be learned from him – Kangaaroo is indeed a great guru! He is well and thriving and rehabilitated as best as we can. What more can I ask for?

About the animal

Bonnet macaque (Macaca radiata) is a species of macaque found only in South India.

It is diurnal (meaning active during the day) and arboreal (meaning living in the trees).

It is terrestrial (meaning living on land), but is also a strong swimmer.

It is an omnivore and lives on fruits, nuts, seeds, flowers, cereals, and some insects like grasshoppers. However, nowadays, because it is so close to humans, it also eats human food.

It gets its name from the cap-like hair on its head that resembles a bonnet.

Fun-fact: it is a very social animal, and much more laidback and carefree compared to other more aggressive macaques

Individuals tend to remain in the troop they were born in.

<u>Why is it in danger?</u>

Numbers have dropped dramatically – a study showed that the number has halved since 2003 in just over a decade.

Urbanization is the main culprit, since reduced canopy and changed landscapes is a drastic change to its habitat

It is often captured and used as a pet, or hunted and sold for road shows.

It often gets electrocuted since it tries to use transmission wires to move about.

It often is treated as a menace and either killed, or moved, which is fatal due to stress.

It is also under attack from the Rhesus macaque, a more aggressive species

3. WHO'S MONITORING THE MONITOR?

Bengal Monitor Lizard (*Varanus bengalensis*)

The jungle in the night is a scary place, but not for those who know the terrain intimately. A lone figure slinks between the trees without a sound, heading towards a marshy bit of wasteland that is dotted with rocks. Once he has reached his destination, he pulls out a thin wire snare from under his shawl. He hesitates and looks around, trying to choose the right spot. The lack of light is not an obstacle as he bends and sets up the snare, for he has done this a thousand times. A few minutes later, he disappears into the night.

The next day, late in the morning, when the sun has climbed the sky and has embraced the earth in a blanket of heat, a little dragon emerges. A dragon? No, not really a dragon! It is a monitor lizard, and it bears an uncanny resemblance to a small dragon. Being cold-blooded, it is still sluggish from the chill of the night, and is looking for a place to bask in the sunlight and warm up. It crawls on the rocks, searching for just the right spot. But when it does find that sweet spot, it is too late. The snare has sprung, the wire has trapped it, and as it flails trying to free itself, it only gets entangled even more. It is a losing battle, *and when the hunter arrives later that day, he finds exactly what he wants.*

The centre is abuzz, because the forest officials have come in today. Forest officials are true heroes, for they are the guardians of our forests. They patrol our jungles, and try their best to keep the areas safe for the wildlife that roam these spaces. They also are constantly on the lookout for poachers. Poachers are hunters who catch and/or kill animals illegally. They are a real threat to wildlife, because many of the animals they catch or kill are endangered species. You may have heard of elephants being killed for their tusks which are made of ivory, or tigers being hunted for their claws and skin. There is a world-wide trade in such forbidden items, and it is very difficult to catch the poachers. I really wish the poachers would turn over a new leaf, and actually work to protect the animals, because they have such an incredible amount of knowledge about wildlife: where exactly the animals roam, what they eat, when they sleep, when they have babies, and so much more. They unfortunately use all this information to capture and sell animal parts. Poachers are now so technically savvy that they can even read up research papers on the net and make use of that information in their work. What a pity they don't use this to protect the animals instead!

Forest officials are regular visitors to our centre, since they drop off the injured animals they have seized from poachers. The police too often come in to hand over the wounded animals they have seized during a raid. Both forest officials and the police do a tremendous amount of work tracking down poachers, and often catch them when they are just about to make a sale of the animal or animal parts. Once the poachers have been caught, there is a long process of gathering evidence and producing the same in court, in order to convict them. Indian laws are quite strong when it comes to wildlife, and there are fines and prison sentences to be faced if someone is caught poaching. I have often been called into court as an expert to testify about the status of the animal when it was brought into our centre, and to answer other technical questions. So, I am on the alert today.

"Here you go, ma'am," says one of the forest officials, and empties a gunny sack on the table.

I blink my eyes in disbelief.

Have you ever seen a movie where the villain kidnaps someone? The hostage usually has his or her hands tied behind her back, and the feet are bound together.

The four monitor lizards that lie on the table are tied up exactly like this. Their forelimbs are tied together, and their hind limbs too are tied together. Their tails are looped back, so that they serve like a handle to a bag.

But what really takes me aback is that the tails are so skinny! That means these monitor lizards have been in captivity for so long without being fed, that they are on the verge of succumbing to starvation.

You're probably wondering how skinny tails tells me all this. Let me explain, taking the human body as an example.

We are all familiar with the main food groups – carbohydrates (like potatoes and rice), proteins (like fish and nuts), and fats (like butter and oil). When we eat these foods, our body digests them and converts them into glucose, which gives us the energy to go about our daily work. Our body also has this wonderful mechanism of turning any extra food into fat and storing them for the future. It is like when you buy an extra bag of chips and keep it in a secret place to eat late at night, when your parents won't scold you!

When we starve, either because we are on a diet, or because there is really no food around for various reasons such as poverty, war, or isolation, our body retrieves the stored fat and converts it into glucose. That is why people can go without food for days without collapsing completely. We will die very soon without water, but we can survive without food!

The monitor lizard does something similar. But it also aestivates. You might have heard about bears hibernating during the winter, when they kind of doze off and wake up only when spring arrives. Aestivation is somewhat similar to this, and monitor lizards, among other species, use this to tide over inhospitable conditions, especially extreme temperatures. Or, as in the case of my hapless patients, getting captured and being starved. The monitor lizard enters into a state of almost complete inactivity, and so uses very little energy to survive. This prolongs the period over which it can stay alive without feeding.

The fact that the monitor lizards dumped before me have such skinny tails means that, despite aestivating, they had to use up all the fat deposits in their tails, so now, they are essentially starving to death.

How can people be so inhuman? I feel a surge of anger rising within me, and I tamp it down. After all, I have loads of work to do. I have to take photos, record exactly in which state the monitor lizards were found, how injured they are, and the exact nature of the injuries. I need to make sure that I capture all the relevant information, in case I need to testify in court. I have my work cut out for me.

I examine the lizards carefully. Right now, I am not at risk of being attacked, because the poor creatures don't have an ounce of energy left, and they are quite still. The limbs of all the four lizards are in bad shape, which is to be expected. Tying the limbs up so tightly and for such a long period hampers circulation to the digits (which is what the fingers and toes are called), and the digits will likely just fall off.

There are so many things that need to be done – treat the lizards for their infections and injuries, dress their wounds regularly till they are healed, restore circulation to the limbs, feed them so that they are back to their normal weight, and only then will we be in a position to release them to the wild.

You might be a bit puzzled by now. When a lizard is spotted in your home, it is normally greeted with shrieks of horror and chased away. Why on earth would anyone want to capture these monitor lizards then, which are lizards on a much bigger and more horrifying scale?

The truth is, monitor lizards are used extensively in traditional medicine. Its blood and parts are used, oil extracted from it is supposed to possess healing properties, and certain parts resemble a plant root called Tiger's Claw (Martynia annua), which is in great demand. Its meat is also considered a delicacy. No wonder poachers hunt these reptiles down, because people are willing to pay exorbitant prices for their parts.

But the role monitor lizards play in the ecology of the forest is a very vital one. They are one of the scavengers of the jungle, and feast on rotting carcasses left by bigger predators. Without them, the food chain is tipped into imbalance, and that is a dangerous thing. Unfortunately, the population of monitor lizards has been depleted so much that it is now listed as an endangered species in Schedule I of the Indian Wildlife Act.

A month passes. To our sorrow, two of the lizards pass away, unable to survive the aftermath of the terrible trauma they were subjected to. We have treated the other two lizards with antibiotics and other medicines, and regular physiotherapy. They are doing a little better, and it is time to move them to a different enclosure.

Monitor lizards are solitary, nocturnal creatures, and this makes continuing the treatment more challenging now. Just like other reptiles such as the snake, monitor lizards are extremely sensitive to vibrations. Walking with thudding footsteps or talking loudly makes them very alert, and ready to attack.

Monitor lizards have really sharp but small teeth, so while they can bite, they can't do much harm. The tail is used as a whip-like weapon, much like the crocodile. The claws are much more effective: they are long and sharp, have great grip, and can inflict quite severe damage. There is even a popular folk story related to this. Ghorpad is what the monitor lizard is known as in Maharashtra, and since its legendary leader apparently scaled a fort wall using a monitor lizard tied to a rope (because of the excellent grip of the claws), his clan got the name Ghorpade!

When we approach one of the monitor lizards, we have to be very, very quiet. Once we are very close to the animal, the boys throw a cloth on the lizard's head so that the senses of sight and smell are dampened. I wear thick gloves so that clawing and biting are ineffective. The physiotherapy session begins. I gently rotate one limb after another several times, first in the clock-wise direction, and then in the anti-clockwise direction. This ensures circulation to all parts of the limbs. We also bathe the animal in infra-red rays for a specific period every day, which is done by a machine that just needs plugging in.

The food is another problem altogether. Their favourite diet is rotting, stinky meat which is just at the right stage of decomposing. We nearly gag every time we have to toss the food into the enclosure, but the lizards obviously consider it quite a feast, because when we return in the morning, the food is all gone. This is great because healthy appetites mean that the lizards are recovering well.

We also notice another happy development. The lizards are exploring their enclosures (when we are not looking, of course), and trying to escape! We find the wires of the enclosure sometimes bent because of repeated nudges with their snouts. This is wonderful because only a healthy animal will be looking for escape routes; an invalid animal will just lie where it has been left. We sometimes even hear low growls in the night, which is heartening.

Three months have now passed since they were first dumped on my table. The two survivors are completely recovered and fit for releasing in the wild. It's time to say good-bye. The boys take the two monitor lizards deep into the jungle and let them down. After a brief hesitation, the two lizards scurry away and disappear.

My work is done, and I am happy. This is what I've always dreamed of doing. Isn't it awesome?

<u>About the animal</u>

- Bengal Monitor Lizard (Varanus bengalensis) also called common Indian monitor, is found in the Indian subcontinent, along with much of Southern Asia.

- It is mainly terrestrial (meaning living on the ground), though the young ones are more arboreal (meaning living in trees).

- It has a varied diet, eating everything from insects to frogs and even rats. It also feeds on carrion (decaying flesh of dead animals).

- It can move rapidly on the ground, climb well, and also swim well.

- Fun-fact: by flicking its long and sensitive tongue repeatedly while moving its head from side to side, it "tastes" its environment.

- When fighting, it makes a hissing noise and puffs up its upper body to appear larger.

Why is it in danger?

- The Bengal Monitor Lizard is one of the animals protected under the Indian Wildlife Act of 1972, under Schedule 1.

- It is often targeted by poachers.

- It is captured and its parts and blood are used for medicinal purposes, while its meat is treated as a delicacy.

4. COFFEE CAT

Asian palm civet cat (*Paradoxurus hermaphroditus*)

The traffic has come to a grinding halt. This isn't unusual, because this is one of Bangalore's busiest intersections, and it is already part of the urban myth, with several jokes and memes about the traffic jams at this junction. However, today's gridlock is not because of accidents, unruly drivers, or vehicles that have broken down.

"That's a leopard cub, I tell you!"

"Really?"

"Well, it doesn't look like a regular house kitten, does it?"

"That's not a leopard cub by any stretch of imagination."

"Then what is it? If you know so much, go ahead and tell us."

The small, trembling black bundle of fur is oblivious to the furore it has created. It is frozen and numb with fear. It cowers from the swirl of petrol and diesel fumes and dust, the roaring of vehicle engines an assault on its ears, the yelling and shouting of concerned but clueless people surrounding it a completely alien world. It needs to escape, to go back to its quiet habitat with rustling trees and chirping birds. But that seems impossible right now, for there is no way out.

"No, this is definitely not a leopard cub," I confirm.

"Then what is it?" The cops who have brought in the fugitive to our centre are curious, for they have never seen anything like this creature before.

I sigh. "It is called a civet cat," I explain. "It's not really a cat, but that's what it is called. It is actually closer to the mongoose. It is a wild animal and you can find these civet cats mostly in the Western Ghats."

The cops look a bit confused.

"If it is not a cat, then why did we find it in the city?" they ask. "Did it escape from the forest?"

I laugh. "It did escape, but not from the forest. It was most probably trapped by poachers and was probably being transported through the city, when it escaped."

"But won't it be kept in a cage? How can it escape?"

"Poachers are very clever. If they use a cage, it can arouse suspicion. So they probably used just a plain old cardboard box to transport it. This baby civet must have found a hole or something through which it escaped, probably when the traffic had halted."

"But why would they capture such a creature? It's too small to eat. Is it used for something else then?"

"Yes. It is used for coffee," I reply, and I receive a look of utter bafflement.

If you are baffled too, let me explain.

You will probably find this explanation a bit gross, so I'm giving you fair warning.

I'm sure you've heard of all sorts of coffee like Arabica and Robusta, and so on. Now, one of the gourmet coffees of the world is Kopi Luwak, originating in Indonesia and the

Philippines. This coffee is very expensive and can cost you around three thousand rupees for a single cup!

How is this coffee made? This is where it gets a bit gross. In the wild, the civet cat eats the coffee cherries. These cherries do not get completely digested, so they are excreted out by the civet cat. The digestive juices impart a distinctive flavour to the coffee beans, and these beans are used to make Kopi Luwak.

Of course, we can trust humans to take things to the extreme. Because of how lucrative this coffee is, entrapment of these civet cats is rampant. They are force-fed the coffee cherries, and the beans harvested from the trapped animals is sold.

However, what is forgotten is that civet cats are actually omnivorous, and the coffee cherries that they eat in the wild just forms a small part of their diet. Trapped civet cats do not have this luxury and because they are fed only the coffee cherries for the most part, they suffer a great deal from malnutrition. Add this to the stress of captivity where they can no longer live their normal lives, it is no wonder that the civet cats are traumatized completely.

As an interesting side note, African civet cats also produce a strong-smelling secretion called musk, and they are trapped for this also.

When I begin to examine my patient, I find several positive factors. For one, the baby civet is not so young that it will get imprinted if we hand-feed it. Imprinting basically means that a newly born animal learns from its parents about the habits of its species. You might have seen some videos where a cat thinks it is a dog and tries to behave like one. When the baby animal is handled by a different species, it learns the habits of that species and begins to behave like that.

The baby civet is severely dehydrated and under great stress. We will need to hand-feed it initially till it becomes a little more independent. It does not have any visible injuries or wounds, so that is a good thing, for it reduces the danger of infections.

The other good thing is that it is not drunk!

Civet cats are also called toddy cats for a good reason. They love to scale palm trees and eat the fermented fruit, which is exactly like alcohol for humans. When they get drunk on this fermented fruit, they slip off the trees and land in the mud below, making a fine mess of themselves. They are also extremely lethargic and cannot run away if humans spot them. I have treated a few such civet cats before, and they are drowsy and uncoordinated. But when the effects of the fermented fruits wear off the next day, they can become quite aggressive and difficult to treat. In most cases, I just let them settle down and then release them into the wild.

This little civet will only need plenty of quiet time and restorative fluids for it to recover completely. So, after a thorough examination, we place it in a quiet, clean enclosure for observation. Since it is not so young that it needs only milk, we ensure that it is supplied a steady diet of fruit, fish, and meat, and it is left completely undisturbed.

Civet cats are nocturnal, so the little one spends the entire day sleeping, but begins to stir at night. A couple of weeks later, we shift it to a more appropriate enclosure that has mud on the ground and branches to climb on. It needs very little human intervention to heal itself from its traumatic experience.

As I mentioned earlier, the civet cat is a not a true cat, meaning it is not a feline. So if you ever find one, you should leave it alone.

We often think that wild animals are just like our domesticated animals, and with a little love and cuddling, we can tame them too. However, wild animals can be quite dangerous, not just because they can bite or attack unexpectedly, but also because they can house bacteria and viruses that are extremely dangerous to humans. When wild animals are held captive, they begin shedding due to stress, and this includes micro-organisms that we are not even familiar with. When these micro-organisms jump to humans from the wild animals, we could end up seriously affected with unrecognizable diseases. We could even end up with a global pandemic that affects millions of people across the world!

Our baby civet recovers very well indeed, and shows a good amount of nocturnal activity, which is always welcome. It is difficult to believe that six months have already passed, and our baby has now become what we call a sub-adult. The enclosure where it is housed has a tree, and we observe the little one constantly looking for gaps through which it can escape. This is good news indeed, for it looks like she (for it is indeed a female) cannot wait to be free. We need to go through official channels, so we promptly send off a letter to the forest department requesting for permission to release our guest. Once we receive the go-ahead, we make arrangements to leave a tiny "accidental" gap in the enclosure. It is like a trap-door and will be open only during the night.

Then we wait. Will she take the bait? What do you think?

Naturally, our little lady discovers the escape route during her nocturnal exploration. It is just a matter of minutes before she pushes through the gap and disappears into the canopy of darkness.

This is exactly what the purpose of my work is, and I am delighted. Another animal rescued, rehabilitated, and released back to the wild. Every single one counts.

About the animal

- Asian palm civet cat (Paradoxurus hermaphroditus) also called common palm civet, or toddy cat, is found in the Indian subcontinent, along with much of Southern Asia.

- It is both terrestrial (meaning living on the ground) and arboreal (meaning living in trees), and is usually solitary.

- It has omnivorous, and eats berries and other fruit, honey and coffee, and as the name suggests, palm, apart from small insects or mammals.

- It is a slow walker and uses trees for faster movement.

- Fun-fact: it doesn't share its food with anyone, since it likes to be alone.

- It has a long tail that is almost as long as its body.

Why is it in danger?

• The Palm Civet Cat is one of the animals protected under the Indian Wildlife Act of 1972, under Schedule 2.

57

• It is often targeted by poachers, and held in captivity under very poor conditions.

• It is fed coffee beans exclusively to make gourmet coffee, which results in malnutrition, stress, and ultimately, death.

5. THE JOKER

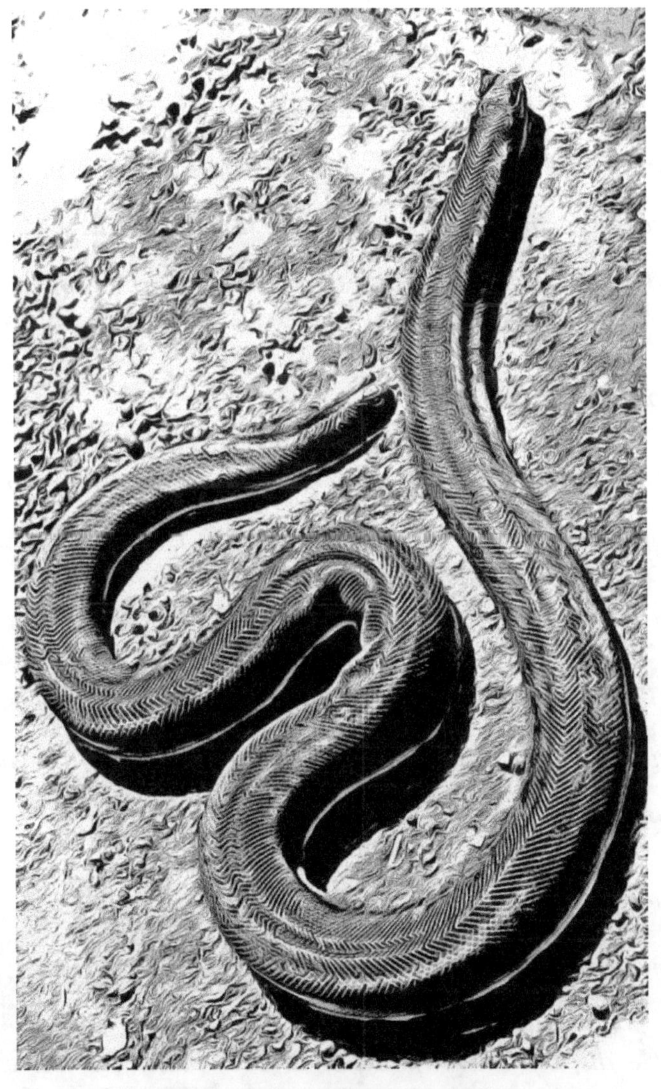

Red Sand Boa (*Eryx johnii*)

"Come one, come all! See this fantastic creature. You will never see anything like it anywhere else in the world!"

The clouds of dust kicked up at the village fair do not deter the families who are out to have a good time. The creaks of the manually operated Ferris wheel and merry-go-round clash with the calls of the vendors selling everything from glittering bangles, sequined sarees, garish toys, and colourful flywheels. Laughing children dart between the legs of the adults, trying to see everything there is on display.

"Come one, come all! If you want to see something truly out of this world, something so dangerous that no one has ever seen before, come quick, come at once!"

The man is surrounded by a crowd that buzzes with curiosity. All eyes are on the basket in front of him, which he opens with a flourish.

"What I have here is a truly amazing snake. Do you know why? It is a two-headed snake! See?"

He displays the two heads of the snake, one on each end, and a collective gasp escapes the stunned gathering.

Little kids clutch at their parents, and newly-wed wives grip their husbands tightly as the snake transfixes them with a sinister smile that resembles the Joker.

If a snake with one head can be deadly, how much deadlier can a two-headed snake be?

If you are shuddering and actually wondering if a two-headed snake is deadlier than a one-headed snake, let me hasten to clear up some misconceptions.

First of all, the Red Sand Boa is definitely not two-headed. It has got just one head, like all other snakes. It is a thick snake, and the tail is almost as thick as the body. The nose of the snake is shovel-shaped, but the tail is also blunt as opposed to being tapered. This is why it is often mistaken to have two heads.

Secondly, the Red Sand Boa is a non-venomous snake. For those interested in details, there is a difference between being poisonous and being venomous. Both poison and venom are harmful to the human body. Poison is usually ingested or absorbed through the skin, such as eating a poisonous fruit or touching a poisonous substance. Venom is injected into the human body through a bite or a sting. Since snakes stun their prey using their venom by biting them, they are called venomous and not poisonous.

However, the Red Sand Boa is actually harmless because it does

not have any venom. In fact, it is a rather shy creature, burrowing into the sand and hiding there, venturing out only at night. In the wild, the Red Sand Boa is often found near water bodies. The soil around such water bodies is loose enough to burrow itself in. Rats and frogs will also be plentiful in the vicinity, which makes hunting easy for the snake. It moves rather sluggishly, so it is very easy to catch if at all spotted. It is very secretive, and since it is nocturnal, it is not very easy to spot.

The Red Sand Boa that lies before me today looks almost dead.

It is not surprising, considering how traumatic its experience has been. It is apparent that it has been used as an attraction in village fairs, because the tail has some markings. These markings are clearly man-made. There are two circles for eyes and a wider curve below, shaped like a smile. On closer examination, it appears to me that these markings have actually been burnt into the skin, using some sort of a flame. The burnt skin has peeled off and the paler flesh underneath is now visible, making the tail look like a face.

And there it is – the fantastic two-headed snake.

I sigh in despair. There is no telling what forms of torture human beings will invent to inflict on helpless animals.

However, this is actually mild compared to some of the other cases I have witnessed.

Believe it or not, there is actually a widespread superstition that wherever the Red Sand Boa is found, buried treasure lies hidden there. This leads to charlatans using this snake to deceive people. They first burrow the snake in the sand at a predetermined location, and then lead the believers to the spot! Of course, a hefty fee is charged and the cheats escape long before the scam is uncovered. It helps that the Red Sand Boa is harmless and slow to move, so catching it again is not very difficult.

Since the snake can be captured quite easily, it is often traded in order take advantage of this superstition. The price of the snake is determined by its weight, and so unscrupulous people actually force-feed metal ball bearings to the snake to increase its weight so that they can charge a fortune. The poor snake can actually choke and die on these metal balls! Sometimes, metal detectors have to be used to check if metal balls are lying within the snake, and we have to surgically remove them from within. The metal ball bearings are often filthy, greasy, and shoved down the snake's throat forcefully. Alternatively, an incision is made, the metal ball bearings are inserted just below the skin, and then stitched up by local quacks who do not maintain any hygiene standards while doing so. This

can lead to choking, blocking of the gut, sepsis, or infection, often resulting in death. How awful is that!

Fortunately (relatively speaking) in the case of this snake, after a thorough examination, it appears to me that the injuries are not very severe. No vital organs have been punctured, and there are no bleeding wounds, so that is a good sign. As long as I keep the burnt marking areas clear of infection, and treat the snake for dehydration and stress, I think it will recover well. The course of treatment will include some broad-spectrum antibiotics, painkillers, and fluids for treating the dehydration. Fluids are normally given based on the body weight of the snake. I will need to warm a syringe and inject the fluids just under the skin in the subcutaneous layer, so that they can get distributed throughout the body.

When a snake is injured, it can also go into aestivation for recovery. Aestivation is basically going into a more or less inactive state, so that energy is conserved for only vital requirements. The Red Sand Boa needs a bed of soil that it can burrow into. The soil needs to be cleaned regularly so that the snake does not pick up any other infections. A bowl of water is provided. No food is provided as the snake has to be given live prey like rats. The prey can smell the blood and pus leaking from the wounds, and can try to escape by biting and injuring the boa, which is already sluggish, weak, and stressed. Snakes also usually do not eat in captivity, so I only give fluids to maintain body condition.

The reptile is then left completely undisturbed. This is very important because too much handling can negatively impact the snake. Too much noise and vibration will disturb it and increase its stress level, which will again hinder its recovery.

We have a room in the centre that contains several wooden containers, which are called vivariums or snake boxes. They have mesh walls and a lid which can be opened. They are often lined with newspapers so that the snakes can lie under them undisturbed. Cloth coverings shroud the containers to keep the light out.

Our patient is placed in one of these boxes. Since the Red Sand Boa is cold-blooded, it is important that the temperature of its environment be regulated. When it gets too cold, it is not unusual to place a heating pad in the container, so that the snake can curl up on it and keep warm.

After about forty-five days of careful monitoring and care, we are greeted with a welcome sight. The Red Sand Boa has begun shedding! Snakes usually moult, or shed their skin regularly, when they are healthy. The period between two moultings varies from species to species. It indicates to us that our guest is well on its way to a complete recovery.

The second moulting happens even quicker. We also notice another encouraging thing: our snake has been using its powerful snout shaped head to push against the mesh, almost creating a hole in it, in a bid to escape. This brings us a lot of cheer because this indicates that it is almost ready for release back into the wild.

It takes at least a couple of months before our Red Sand Boa is certified as fit for release. The skin on the tail markings has healed completely.

Birds are roosting on the trees and stars are becoming visible in the rapidly darkening skies, when our guest is let down gently near the edge of a water body. It takes a few seconds before it slithers off and burrows itself, disappearing rapidly from sight.

We don't really need hidden treasures in the form of gold or gems. What we really need is to leave the Red Sand Boa alone, and treasure it for itself.

About the animal

- Red Sand Boa (Eryx johnii) also called Indian Sand Boa, is found in the dry areas of the Indian subcontinent. It is the largest sand boa in the world.

- It is nocturnal and spends most of its time burrowed under the earth.

- It feeds on rodents, lizards and even other snakes.

- It is harmless and non-venomous.

- Fun-fact: it is ovoviviparous, meaning the eggs are hatched within the body of the parent.

- It can grow anywhere between two to three feet in length.

Why is it in danger?

- The Red Sand Boa is one of the animals protected under the Indian Wildlife Act of 1972, under Schedule 4.

• It is losing its habitat due to rapid expansion of human settlements.

• It is often exhibited as a two-headed snake, and it is also used to identify sites for hidden treasures based on a prevalent superstition. So it is illegally traded quite widely.

6. THE FAULT IN THE STARS

Indian Star Tortoise (*Geochelone elegans*)

The farmer straightens up, wincing as his back twinges with pain. He looks up at the bright blue sky, with nary a cloud in sight, and he sighs deeply. This time too, it promises to be a difficult season, and a poor harvest means the life of his family will only take a turn for the worse.

A voice startles him and he turns to see a man who is well-dressed and looks like an affluent city dweller.

"Tough times, eh?" The visitor asks, and the farmer hesitates, then nods.

The man muses for a minute, then whips out a photo from his shirt pocket.

"Seen any of these around?" He asks, showing the photo to the farmer, who peers at it. His face brightens with recognition.

"Yes, yes!" He nods. "I've seen quite a few there," he replies, waving a hand towards the edge of his farm.

"If you can catch them for me, I'll pay you ten bucks for each," the man says.

The farmer hesitates before he replies cautiously. "Twenty-five."

"Twenty."

The farmer shrugs, then leads his guest to a corner of the farm where there are a couple of large stones. He pushes one of the stones, and watches as his guest breaks into a delighted grin.

That's an easy two hundred rupees he's made in under five minutes. Perhaps his luck is turning after all.

We watch as the officials empty the sack, and the contents rain down on the ground. This is unbelievable. These are living beings, for heaven's sake! Do people have no moral compasses at all?

I am looking at literally a heap of Star Tortoises.

The Star Tortoise, as the name suggests, is a tortoise that stays on land. It gets its name from its beautiful shell, which has lovely star patterns on it. What a brilliant way to camouflage itself, as it wanders along the dappled floor of the forest, its shell merging seamlessly with the patches of sunlight that stream through the leaves on the trees!

Unfortunately, this star pattern has also attracted humans to the tortoise. The pattern is considered a good luck charm. In Karnataka, the animal is popularly known as *Nakshatra Aame* (literally Star Tortoise), and is often purchased by people who believe it will bring them luck.

Good luck for people sadly means bad luck for the Star Tortoises. They are caught and traded illegally, and sold to people who believe they will get lucky. Not so fast however, for if you are found in possession of such a tortoise, you can actually face criminal charges and have the bad luck to be imprisoned!

Here it might make sense to clarify on a very common confusion regarding the difference between tortoises and turtles, and the less frequently used term, terrapins. They are all classified under the order Testudines. This order was formerly Chelonia, so Chelonia is also often used to refer to these shelled reptiles as a whole.

A Tortoise is terrestrial, meaning it lives on land and not in water.

A Terrapin is amphibious, meaning it can live on both land and in water.

A Turtle is aquatic, meaning it lives only in the water.

It is important to know the difference between these because very often people mistake one for the other, and could easily kill the animal by placing it in water when it is terrestrial, or forcing it to live on land when it is aquatic. All three are air breathing, but are found and live mainly on land, or water, or both land and water.

Coming back to the miserable heap that lies on the ground, there are thirty-two Star Tortoises in total. They've been carried around like regular luggage. Just like when you unpack your suitcase, and all the clothes at the bottom are wrinkled and crushed, the unlucky tortoises at the bottom have been crushed by the weight of the ones on top. Some have been suffocated and are now definitely prone to, if not already affected by respiratory infections.

The good thing about tortoises is that they are precocious –
as soon as they are born, they begin to move around and are
able to take care of themselves (unlike say, human babies,
who take a few years before they are able to function
independently). Also, since they are reptiles, they are more
resilient. They are able to sink into a state of aestivation
when conditions are inhospitable, and will do just the bare
minimum to keep alive. This really helps them to survive the
horrific conditions under which they are transported after
capture, for they are often packed densely into sacks and
boxes, with little or no care for their welfare.

It is however a challenge to inspect and treat tortoises for
they have extremely fast reflexes and withdraw into their
shells at even the slightest hint of a threat.

My priorities in treating these thirty-two tortoises are very
clear.

First, I will segregate them into groups after an initial inspection, based on how good or bad their condition is.

The good ones will require just a week or so of observation before we let them go back to their natural habitat. They will need to eat properly, move about without issues, and their reflexes need to be on point. We need to hydrate them adequately, give them sunlight and food and room to move around, and keep them sufficiently warm. We will start with grated carrot and then move on to more leafy vegetables for their nutrition.

It is heartening to note that at least twenty of the tortoises are in good shape to be released soon. So we get all the paperwork started, so that the release happens as early as possible. The remaining tortoises have various issues that we need to work through.

When the tortoise pulls its head into the shell, it is quite literally holding its breath. The shell is a small space, and there is no room for the lungs to expand when breathing. Since the ones at the bottom have almost been suffocated, it is not a surprise that they have developed respiratory infections. Added to this, the stress that they have undergone makes recovery slower.

One of the first things I check is to see if the reflexes are hampered. If the tortoise does not withdraw immediately into its shell upon being poked gently, it is a clear indication that it is not doing well.

The other things I check for is if the eyes are closed and oozing, or if the nasal cavities are blocked with discharge. These are again very clear symptoms of respiratory infections.

Apart from the usual broad-spectrum antibiotics that we treat the animals with, I also need to do nebulization and/or steaming. Yes, you read that right! It is very similar to what we do when we get a cold. The nebulisation is done with medications added in a steamer to soften nasal secretions, and clear the passages, and also reduce the nasal secretions for full healing. This is done where the tortoise is, and we cover the box with a towel, so that there is a sauna effect, and the steam helps the nasal passages clear up.

We keep them under observation in smaller boxes where the environment is more controlled and mud is cleaned every week. The mud is changed to reduce the microbial and parasitic infections shed in the faeces and urine. Once I feel they are recovered sufficiently, we begin to move them into bigger enclosures where they can move out freely on the natural ground and also be exposed to sunlight, which is very important. They are heliotherms, which means they require sunlight daily, and which is the best natural medicine.

The tortoises, resilient as always, show excellent improvement, and within two months, they are back to their usual selves. The rainy season is the best time to release them, since they will have enough food with the forest greening. However, we don't necessarily wait for rainy season because they are part of our dry, deciduous forests and so are capable of handling dry spells too. Our main aim is to release the healthy ones as soon as possible because in crowded enclosures, living and eating and excreting together increases the chances of picking up infection greatly.

Soon it is time to let them go, and we do so in the heart of the forest. We wish them good luck and hope they don't get caught again. They amble out and disappear into the landscape.

Wishing upon a Star (Tortoise) has never felt so good!

About the animal

- The Indian Star Tortoise (Geochelone elegans) is found in India, Pakistan and Sri Lanka.

- It lives mostly in dry areas and scrub forests.

- It is very shy and does not like being handled.

- It is mostly a herbivore and should never be fed meat.

- Fun-fact: its shape makes it easy to make itself upright if turned upside down!

- Its lifespan is anywhere between thirty to eighty years.

Why is it in danger?

- The Indian Star Tortoise is one of the animals protected under the Indian Wildlife Act of 1972, under Schedule 1. It was moved under this

Schedule in December 2022 due to rampant poaching and lots of seizures by the authorities.

- It is treated as a good luck charm and is in great demand, and hence it is traded illegally.

- Both poachers and people who own the Star Tortoise as a pet are unaware that trading is illegal.

- Even young Star Tortoises are not safe from poaching, and so the population is dwindling very fast.

7. MOOSHIE THE WILD CHILD

Indian Grey Mongoose (*Herpestes edwardsii*)

"Amma! Amma! Come and see what I found!"

The little girl appears at the threshold of the hut, eyes sparkling and cheeks flushed with excitement.

Her mother laughs, wipes her wet hands on her sari and hurries along behind the skipping child.

"See!" The girl's voice drops to a hush. "It's a baby."

The mother halts next to her daughter, who is sitting on her haunches and pointing at a little grey thing that lies on the ground. It is barely breathing. The girl makes as if to scoop it up into her hands.

"Just leave it, kanna," the mother says in a sharp voice. "It's wild. Don't touch it."

"But...but, if we leave it here, it will die, won't it?" the girl's voice quivers, and her eyes rapidly well up with tears. "We can't just leave it here, Amma. Please!"

The mother sighs. "All right. But you must do as I say, and I will take it to a place where it will be safe, okay?"

The little girl nods, looking serious. All she wants is to save the baby.

"A baby mongoose?" I repeat in disbelief, and my boys nod, grinning.

I sigh. Looks like I now have to don yet another role – that of a baby-sitter!

"Fine," I say. "Let's find out how the kiddo is doing."

The baby mongoose is really tiny, about the length of my palm. She is obviously an infant, probably somewhat slightly older than fifteen days since her umbilical cord wound has healed. She does not have any apparent injuries or wounds that suggest she was mauled by a predator. How she got separated from her mother will remain a mystery.

Her most urgent need is obviously to be fed. I send off my boys to hunt for a really tiny feeding bottle, while I prepare her feed. We can't give her the kind of milk we humans drink such as milk from cows, goats, or buffalos. This milk will be full of hormones and chemicals and may harm the baby more than aid her. So I use formula milk like Lactogen, which is much safer, and prepare it exactly like how I would prepare it for a human baby. I sterilize the feeding bottle and the nipple, dissolve the milk powder in boiled and cooled water, fill up the bottle with the solution, and then I begin to feed her. There is always a danger that she will reject this feed, or that she will not be able to latch on to the nipple and suck – I have experienced this when feeding other wild animals. I only hope that she takes to it for she really needs this feed in order to survive. She is already very weak and hanging on by a thread.

As I position the bottle and gently push it against her mouth, I am relieved to see that she latches on to it almost at once and sucks at it hungrily. She is ravenous, and finishes up the portion in no time. From the way she searches, it is obvious that she would like more, but I can't risk that. I need to wait and see if this feed agrees with her or not. If she rejects it, we are in serious trouble indeed.

A baby monkey has also been brought in, so we decide that these two can keep each other good company. We house both of them side by side in their own baskets, with a stuffed toy in each basket for comfort along with a heat source to ensure that they remain warm.

Mooshie, as I've nicknamed the little mongoose, appears to have taken to the milk beautifully. She digests it well and her poop is a good consistency. I heave a sigh of relief, for this means we are all set for her feeds at least for a week or two.

I feel quite certain that Mooshie has had her mother's milk for the first few days of her existence at least. Any mother's natural milk is full of good things for the baby, which is why there is such an insistence that babies must be breast-fed. One of the good things that gets passed on to the baby are the antibodies. These are the things that fight off infections, and the mother's body will have all the antibodies for whatever infections she has been exposed to in her life. In the first few days, these antibodies are absorbed by the baby through the mother's milk, and they help the baby fight off these infections too, should they ever occur in the future. The baby's immunity is thus at a much higher level if she gets to drink her mother's milk.

Not only does the mother's milk help the baby as I already explained, but you also must have noticed how animal moms often lick their babies repeatedly. This licking is yet another way of protecting their baby. Not only does the licking clean up the baby from all the urine or poop they have excreted, but the saliva also contains certain antiseptic properties, so that the baby remains free of infections. I need to ensure that this kind of cleanliness is maintained for babies under my care too. I need to come up with other alternatives, since I obviously can't lick them!

We need to feed Mooshie every two to three hours, so we draw up a feeding regimen. The quantity of milk is approximately ten percent of the body weight. She has started with just 50ml, but soon the quantity will be much more than that because hopefully, she will start to gain weight.

The feed has to be done under supervision. Why is that, you might wonder? Why can't we just leave a cup of milk in her basket so that she can drink it whenever she wants? Well, for one thing, she can easily bump into the cup and overturn it, and then her basket will be flooded with milk that she will not be able to drink, apart from leaving her wet and shivering from cold. The other reason is that spilled milk can attract insects such as ants. Ants can swarm the basket, and even be so vicious as to attack Mooshie herself! That is definitely something we don't want happening, so we take turns in feeding both Mooshie and her friend – the baby monkey. After the feed, we need to wipe her down so that she doesn't have milk sticking on her body that will attract feasting ants. I also ensure that she is gently wiped all over with a cotton swab dipped in a diluted antiseptic solution at the end of the day, so that she is clean and not prone to catching any infections. We clean the baskets every day, including the stuffed toy that they use for cuddling, replace the newspapers with fresh ones, and just leave the babies to sleep and catch up on their growing.

Mooshie grows by leaps and bounds. Her appetite is healthy and we must soon wean her from the milk. We begin to give her eggs and milk for comfort every now and then, but soon move onto minced beef. We cannot give her chicken or other usual meats, for fear that she will get hooked on to their taste, and when she leaves the centre, she might begin to raid and attack poultry centres just for a taste of chicken! Beef is a safer option, for there is not much chance of her trying to take on and attack full-grown cattle. Of course, in the wild, mongooses have an eclectic diet consisting of all sorts of eggs and hatchlings and so on, which we cannot accurately reproduce in captivity.

We will need to start the process of soft release as soon as we start weaning her off milk and get her onto solids. This will be done by leaving her free to roam around during day and keeping her safe in an enclosure at night.

Mooshie also gets along like fire with her companion, the baby monkey. They begin to play with each other, steal each other's food, and as they grow, they begin to rough-house with each other! It is now indeed a task to keep these two naughty kids out of mischief!

I also begin to take Mooshie out on walks around the centre. The sunshine, with its daily dose of Vitamin D, is essential for her. She begins to monopolize my company, running up to my desk, climbing on my shoulder, insisting that she be petted, and I groom her for the ticks around her eyes and mouth. Her eyes gleam like polished stones; they are sharp and inquisitive and dancing with mischief! I try to be firm with her and put her down and away, but she will have none of it. It makes things worse that I have developed an allergy owing to contact with her, and am even taking medications for it, but she persists in following me around. Part of it might be because of imprinting, since I handled her when she was still a baby, but most of it is probably because she is just a regular drama queen!

Her behaviour becomes worse when we move her into a bigger enclosure after around three months. As part of the soft release process, she is free to move around during the day, but she shrieks and wails when we put her in the enclosure at evening for the night. She literally throws tantrums, creating a racket by whining out loudly, and makes her displeasure loudly known. She even plays so rough with her baby friend that other monkeys at the centre mistake her for a predator attacking their kind, and send out alarm calls! She waits for the sound of my bike as I enter the centre – that's the cue for her melodrama to begin.

All of that suddenly changes over a weekend, as if a switch has been flipped. On a Monday, when I return to the centre, I expect her to come scampering towards me as usual, demanding my attention. However, she is nowhere to be found. I begin to get worried as the day progresses, and still there is no sign of her.

"There she is!" One of my boys shouts in excitement late in the afternoon. And sure enough, Mooshie is back. But she is not rushing to me. She is more aloof, and I spot some scratches. Has she been out in the wild? After all, there are wild mongooses around, and it is not impossible for her to have encountered one or more of them. Has she got into a scrap with one of them? Was she attacked? I am worried, but at the same time, I am careful not to get too involved. It is ultimately our goal that she is released into the wild. She needs to be able to stand her ground and live her life there, amongst her own kind. Any intervention on my part now will only hamper this development, even if I wish to just give her any medical attention she might need.

I observe her quietly over the next few weeks. After a month of this routine, she becomes quieter and more secretive. Her drama queen behaviour has receded so much that it has almost disappeared. She pops out in the morning as if to say hi but then disappears during the day when left free. Also she begins to leave most of her feed uneaten, just pecking on it. This is a clear sign that that she is not hungry and has already eaten on her sojourns.

She is missing for longer periods of time, she is more reclusive and inhibited around humans, and all signs point to her mingling with her own kind in the jungle around the centre. It is a good thing, for she is learning to be her natural self, absorbing all the skills required for surviving.

I do miss her boisterous presence though. She has a distinguishing cut on her tail, no doubt from some skirmish with some wild creature, and I use that to identify her any time I see a mongoose dashing across the ground. I sometimes even call out "Mooshie!" in the fond hope that she might recognize my voice. But it is as it should be – she is off living her own mongoose life, and it is time we prepare for her release. Finally one day, she doesn't show up in the evening feed time, and from then on, we only see her off and on. It's time for the official release request to be sent to the Range Forest Officer (RFO) for release and documentation of the same.

Nine months – that's how long it's taken for my little Mooshie to grow up and seek her own adventures out in the big bad world. I have no doubt that she will live well and

long, and build her own family. But wherever she goes, she

will always have a piece of my heart with her.

About the animal

- The Indian Grey Mongoose (Herpestes edwardsii) is found in Indian subcontinent and in many parts of Asia.

- It lives in a variety of habitats, including forests, open scrublands, and even close to human dwellings.

- It is bold and curious, but very careful.

- It is well-known for its ability to fight with venomous snakes.

- Fun-fact: it can apparently distinguish four colours!

- Its lifespan is anywhere between seven to twelve years.

Why is it in danger?

- The Indian Grey Mongoose is one of the animals protected under the Indian Wildlife Act of 1972, under Schedule 2.

- Fine brushes made out of its hair are in great demand, and hence it is traded illegally.

- According to some sources, at least 50 animals have to be killed for 1 kg of mongoose hair.

- Very little is unfortunately known about poaching of the Indian Grey Mongoose.

8. FOXED

Indian Fox (*Vulpus bengalensis*)

The little pup scrambles through the dry grass, his tiny heart palpitating wildly.

There's no sign of either its mom or dad. Where could they have gone? Did he wander off too far? Or did he take a nap for too long?

His small head is scrambling to figure out what happened.

He turns around in a circle. Can he find his way home to his den? His sister will be waiting, won't she? The grass looks shorter that way, maybe he can take a look? He stumbles, trying to find his footing on the pebbles and stones that make the ground so uneven.

A sudden crackling of twigs underfoot makes him freeze.

"What do we have here?"

The rumbling voice sounds like thunder and he breaks into such shivers that he feels his heart will just explode, as he is scooped up by a giant hand.

"Calm down, little chap. There's nothing to worry. Let's get you somewhere safe."

The soothing voice and the gentle fingers stroking his head are somewhat reassuring. But as he is carried away to God knows where, he can only think of his family and how much they will miss him.

"Want to bet? It's a dog. Hundred percent it's a wild dog."

"It doesn't look like a jackal, but it isn't a dog for sure!"

"How do you know?"

I enter the room in the middle of a heated discussion.

"What's going on?" I demand. "And what have we here?"

A little four-legged creature is the centre of attraction. It's obviously a baby, but it isn't new-born by the looks of it. I clap my hands to get the attention of my boys.

"Let's go, boys. You know what to do."

I slip on my gloves and begin a careful physical examination of the canine that has been brought in. No wounds or injuries or bleeding anywhere, which is good. It has its eyes wide open, it is snarling and aggressive, and it is very apparent that it is not used to being handled by people at all. All of this points to it being a wild animal that has somehow ended up in the city.

"So Akka, it is a dog, right?"

I examine the ears carefully, which have a very distinct shape.

"Surprise!" I announce. "This is an Indian fox."

It is not unusual for the Indian fox to be mistaken for a dog. In the forests of India, you can find wild canines like wolves, jackals, wild dogs (dhole) and foxes. Hyenas and caracals are also found. Some are scavengers but most also are very good hunters. As scavengers, they feast on the remains of animals killed by the larger carnivores, and as hunters, they prey on smaller creatures, and are hence are invaluable to the ecology. While wolves are larger, with the average male weighing anywhere between 8.5 to 12.5 kgs, jackals are around 7 kgs, while foxes are the smallest, weighing anywhere between 2.5 to 5.5 kgs.

It is hard to say why this particular pup has been found straying outside its normal habitat. One possible cause is that it has just got lost or separated from its parents. The other scenarios are more dire. Sometimes poisoned meat is scattered by humans to get rid of some other dangerous creatures, such as wild boars which raid and destroy crops, so other carnivores become collateral damage. Perhaps the parents have eaten this poisoned food and died as a result. Another possibility is that the parents have been captured by poachers who will sell the pelt and body parts, which are often used in native medicines and rituals.

One point I often emphasize is to never handle wild animals directly, especially the babies. The obvious reason is that the wild animals could turn around and attack or bite in defence, which is dangerous. But the more important reason is that when we handle the babies directly without gloves, we can transfer bacteria and viruses that are present on our skin and cause infection in them. Also the scent or smell from our hands can rub off on the pups, thereby altering their smell, so reintroduction and reunion with parents will not be successful, since the parents can no longer recognise their pup due to the changed smell. Cuddling the baby may seem to be an act of love from our perspective, but the animal parents will often reject the baby as not one of their own. This could be disastrous for the little one's survival.

So if you ever have to handle any baby animal that is not domesticated, always use gloves or a cloth or some paper. This way, you can safely restore the baby to its parents if the opportunity arises.

Coming back to our little fox pup, since it does not require special medical treatment, I decide that we will minimise its handling and try to preserve its wild behaviour. We house it in an internal enclosure and begin to feed it using diluted milk prepared using milk powder. We do not use cow's milk because it has antibiotics which can affect the pup, and cause diarrhoea, drug resistance, etc. The pup drinks up the milk without a fuss. The next step would be to check if it has been fully weaned and if it has begun on solids. We give it a little minced meat, and it gobbles it up. We settle into a regular routine with minimal interaction, so that it does not get too used to having people around all the time.

We are still not sure if the fox is male or female. It takes time for the sexual characteristics to become apparent, so we will just have to wait and watch. Meanwhile we need to deworm it and douse it with tick powder so that the pup does not become a nice and cosy home for all sorts of ectoparasites.

Deworming is a real challenge. The fox pup does not appreciate being held firmly by the neck, and squirms violently trying to break free. It tries to bite, so the head needs to be held firmly too. The paws have claws which can scratch, so they too have to be held down. The eyes needs to be covered so that it cannot see what is happening. All this elevates the stress in the animal to a great degree, so it is imperative that we give it the medicine as quickly as we can.

After the fox is in position, there is no guarantee it will not spit out or gag on the deworming medicine. So we need to slide the medicine through the side of the mouth, so that it swallows it without any issues. The deworming goes through smoothly, and we leave the pup to recuperate in its enclosure.

Foxes are in general quite shy. They normally stay in pairs and give birth to two to four pups. They don't actively socialize, so if we need our little friend to stay true to its nature, we need to give it privacy and isolation.

So we prepare an enclosure that is inside the centre but far away from our offices, surgery room, and feed cutting room. It is secluded and has minimum human sounds so as to not disturb it. We move the fox there and continue to observe. There's nothing much to see during the day, for foxes are nocturnal. I often just see a curled-up ball of fur in the corner of the enclosure, and it is only the excretions that tell me the state of his health: the faeces indicates whether he is digesting the meat or not, the consistency of the faeces indicates if he is suffering from any constipation or diarrhoea or gut parasites, etc. So I keep track on his health status by keeping a close watch of his urine and faeces.

After about two months, we do a blood test and other basic examinations, which tells us that the pup is a male.

We now need to trigger his hunting instincts. Apart from scavenging, foxes are omnivorous and can eat fruits as well as smaller animals such as insects, rodents, and tiny mammals. They can hunt small birds, and raid nests for eggs, etc. We introduce small live mice and rats into his enclosure so that he can get used to preying on them. I continue observing him with minimal interaction.

After another two months or so, I think he is ready to explore his wild side. I advocate a soft release, where the enclosure is left open, and he is free to roam around and make his own choice on whether to return to the centre, or venture out into the jungle. It takes barely a week for him to choose. He disappears and doesn't return to the enclosure. I am optimistic that he can make it on his own out there in the wild.

One evening, shortly after his disappearance, I wait a little away from enclosure to just check if there is any sign of him. Of course there isn't, and I am about to walk away, when I sense something. From the corner of my eye, I spot him! Beautifully camouflaged by the foliage barely fifteen feet away, he just sits and watches me. Then in a flash, he is gone!

I exhale deeply. It feels surreal. It's almost as if he wanted to reassure me that he was going to be fine.

We don't spot him again, and I pray that he is doing well, wherever he is.

On a related note, I'd like to mention a trend that worries me a lot. In some ways, opening up of jungle resorts to people and their pets puts wild life such as these foxes in more danger. People often think they are showing their love and doing the right thing by taking their pets to the wild, and allowing them to freely run around and play and enjoy themselves.

However, what they forget is that domesticated animals are vaccinated and treated with antibiotics and other medicines whenever they fall ill. Hence, they are more resistant to infections. However, wild animals don't have the luxury of vaccinations or antibiotics and can fall prey to infections that do not affect pets. A pet dog in the jungle would definitely pee or poop there, and wild animals such as foxes, wolves, jackals, and wild dogs could easily pick up these infections. There is no way to figure out if the wild animal survives the infection or dies because of it. By taking our pets to these jungle resorts and other wild places, we are doing untold and unseen damage to the wild life, and we are quite unaware of it unfortunately.

Hopefully my dear Mr. Fox does not face such issues and lives a long and healthy life!

About the animal

- The Indian Fox (Vulpus bengalensis) is found in Indian subcontinent and in parts of Pakistan, Nepal and Bangladesh.

- It prefers dry, deciduous forests where there is scrub, thorn, or short grasslands, and sometimes even close to human dwellings.

- It is crepuscular (active during dawn or twilight), and nocturnal (active during the night).

- It lives in dens and usually as a parent pair (mother and father).

- Fun-fact: it is the smallest wild canid (belonging to Canidae family, like dogs) in India

- Its lifespan is around ten years.

Why is it in danger?

- The Indian Fox is one of the animals protected under the Indian Wildlife Act of 1972, under Schedule 2.

- It is poached for its fine pelt, and it is hunted as part of certain rituals.

- Its body parts are sold for their supposedly medicinal properties.

- The main issue is that the open grasslands are being taken over by humans, and thereby driving them out of their habitat, as well as exposing them to infections carried by domestic pets.

9. CAUGHT IN THE MIDDLE

Indian Pond Terrapin (*Melanochelys trijuga*)

"I don't care! I want a pet!"

The little boy's voice quavers, his lips tremble, and tears fill his eyes.

His mother glances at her husband, and crouches down to embrace her son.

"Our place is too small for a dog, sweetie. And you know you're allergic to cats."

"All my friends have got pets," he sobs into her shoulder.

His father rolls his eyes and shrugs.

"We'll get you a pet soon, don't worry," his mother strokes his back. "Maybe a parrot?"

"I don't want to keep a bird in a cage," the little boy wipes his tears.

"I'm not having birds flying around the house," his father says, and his mother glares at him.

"We'll think of something," she reassures. "Hey, what about a tortoise?"

"Like the hare and tortoise story?" The boy's face lights up. "Oh yes, please! Can we go today and get it?"

"We can go over the weekend. Daddy's busy today," his mother says.

"Can I choose the name?" The boy is jumping up and down in excitement.

"Whatever you want," his mother says, heaving a sigh of relief. She can't bear to see her son shed tears.

"Sure, I'll do whatever I can," I say over the phone.

I'm speaking with a person who has been volunteering at the centre, and we are discussing her neighbour's pet, an Indian Pond Terrapin.

For the purpose of clarity, though the terms are used interchangeably, these are the most accepted generalizations:

Tortoises are completely terrestrial and their shells are typically dome-shaped. They are mainly herbivorous and can grow to very large sizes.

Turtles are completely aquatic, their shells are flat and streamlined for swimming. They are omnivorous, their diet varying from seaweed to jellyfish, and they can also grow to large sizes.

Terrapins are in the middle. They are semi-aquatic and primarily live around freshwater such as ponds and lakes. They are omnivorous, their diet varying from small fish to aquatic plants. They normally do not grow to large sizes.

As mentioned earlier, the term Chelonia is often used to refer to all these shelled reptiles as a whole.

My volunteer says that when she visited her neighbours, she saw their terrapin with a large swelling on its hind leg. Apparently the swelling has been there for quite some time. The vet had taken an X-ray but was rather reluctant to operate on it.

The volunteer recognised that the terrapin was a protected species and persuaded her neighbours that it was in their best interest to give the pet up.

"Bring in their pet to our centre, and I will take a look," I tell her.

About a week later, the animal is brought into the centre in a cardboard box along with the X-ray.

I take a look at my new patient, and I let out a whistle. This is indeed an Indian Pond Terrapin.

Terrapins can be pretty aggressive and can bite with their powerful snapping jaw. They have sharp claws too. Possessing an Indian Pond Terrapin is illegal. I'm not sure how the family managed to get this as a pet for their child.

I arrange for the terrapin to be left in an enclosure with water, basking space, dry areas and plenty of sunlight, along with fish as food, so that I can observe it for at least a week.

I can see the swelling quite clearly. I've examined her physically and the X-ray reveals that she is carrying eggs. The information I gather about her history reveals that she has been kept in a small fish tank with pebbles and grit at the bottom of the tank. She has been fed chappathis and other cooked food eaten by humans, and she has not been exposed to sunlight nor has she had any exercise.

Based on all this and all the research I've done, it looks most likely that this is an "egg bound" condition, meaning that because of poor husbandry and care, she is unable to lay the eggs which have been retained in her body. One such egg might be the cause of the swelling.

But this is just a tentative diagnosis, and I will definitely need to dig deeper, and for that I will require to perform surgery on her.

Surgery on these shelled reptiles is not straight-forward. I cannot just cut open the shell and investigate. There is a small space between the plastron (top shell) and the carapace (bottom), and this is the area in which I will have to operate.

This needs to be a planned surgery and I have to take my time in ensuring that I do it right.

A week later, we are ready to go.

Once my patient is sedated, I make a cut on the hind leg and carefully fold back the layers of skin till I reach the site of the swelling.

I stare at what lies before me – I cannot believe my eyes. The swelling is not because of an egg that she cannot lay. It is because of pebbles!

Small bits of pebbles and gravel are all packed tightly into the space. I recognize them – these pebbles are typically placed at the bottom of an aquarium. This poor creature has literally been eating the pebbles off the floor!

This is directly a consequence of poor diet. The terrapin had been fed a carb-rich diet with things like chappathis, etc. It was craving protein, and had gotten so desperate and deranged that it had begun chewing on the pebbles. Though some amount of the grit would have got excreted naturally, a weak spot in its intestines would have allowed the pebbles to settle down. Gravity would have finished the job, making the spot sag even more, and allow even more pebbles to collect. So much has been collected that the intestine has actually sagged into the hind leg, and hence the visible swelling.

I can understand why the vet had difficulties in diagnosing the issue. Terrapins are wild animals and not so commonly available. Dogs and cats and other pets are easier to diagnose because they are much more customary and there is so much information available about them. An intimate knowledge about the terrapin, its habitat, and its dietary habits is not exactly mainstream.

The swelling is so packed that I actually have to use my finger to loosen some of the material, before I can clear it all out. Once all the foreign matter has been flushed, I need to stitch it all up. I have to suture each layer separately and given that I have a very small area to work in, I have to draw on all my surgical skills to do a neat job.

Once that is done, I place a pressure bandage on the surgical wound to prevent recurrence, and I ensure that she gets a dose of painkillers and antibiotics. We don't give her any solid food, for we need the intestine to recover completely without working too much. We need to keep her dry to ensure proper healing of the wound. Since her shell might dry out completely, and that is not desirable, we keep a wet cloth on her shell and change it twice a day so that it remains moist. We keep her on intracoelomic fluids (fluids injected directly into the body cavity) to give rest to her intestines.

After fifteen days, it is time to remove the stitches. Once again, the terrapin is sedated. It is required because these creatures have such sharp reflexes that it is almost impossible to work with them when they are conscious. The reflex to withdraw into the shell is immediate and extremely rapid and makes working on her unfeasible.

She is then shifted into an outdoor enclosure that has water and allows her to bask in the sun. I observe her every day and am glad to see that she is thriving. Her appetite has shown improvement, which is a good sign of recovery. Her gait too has improved, not just because the swelling has been removed but also because her feet have got a good grip now on the natural earth.

When kept indoors on mostly tiled floors, tortoises and terrapins cannot find a good grip on the smooth floor. Their claws get deformed, and their gait gets affected as they hobble along. That's why it is so important to research on animals before we bring them home to an environment which is not comfortable for them at all, or feed them an imbalanced diet that is lacking what they really need.

I am happy that the terrapin is where she should be. A few days later, she even goes ahead and lays the eggs!

I update the family with the good news, but also tell them that their pet will not be returned to them, and will instead be released later into the wild.

They are hugely relieved that their pet has recovered fully, embarrassed that they did not know it was a terrapin and therefore could not be kept as a pet, and feel really bad that they did not do their due diligence in educating themselves about their pet and its needs. They promise to do a better job if they get another pet, and are very grateful that their terrapin has regained her health.

I sit back with a sigh of relief, thinking of how we humans tend to interpret everything from our human lens. We attribute human qualities to animals, when we should instead be trying to understand their behaviour. We laugh at a video of a dog presenting its bottom to another dog, but fail to understand that it is common among pack animals to show their leader their most vulnerable part as a sign of submission and friendliness, and that they are not a threat. We think we are showering love on our pets by feeding them all sorts of delicacies and cuddling with them and so on. A better approach to show our love would be to understand their behaviours and habits, and create an environment where they can truly flourish without our constant well-meaning but disruptive interventions.

Our recovered terrapin is all set for release around three to four months later.

We release her near a water body and she ambles away, looking fit and fine, with no trace of discomfort from the surgery.

I certainly hope she lives to a ripe old age!

<u>About the animal</u>

- The Indian Pond Terrapin, also known as the Indian black turtle (Melanochelys trijuga) is native to South Asia.

- It is medium-sized and found around standing water bodies like ponds and artificial water bodies like rice paddies, and sometimes rivers.

- It likes to bask in the sun during the day, and is active during early morning.

- It is an omnivore, and eats anything from aquatic plants to aquatic insects.

- Fun-fact: sometimes the female digs a nest to lay eggs in elephant or rhinoceros dung

- Its lifespan is around forty years.

<u>Why is it in danger?</u>

- The Indian Pond Terrapin is one of the animals protected under the Indian Wildlife Act of 1972, under Schedule 4.

- It is often adopted as an exotic pet even though it is illegal.

- Turtle eggs and meat is considered a delicacy and so it is traded.

- Though it is still widespread, population is dwindling due to increased human settlements and illegal trade.

10. BUCKY'S ESCAPE

Blackbuck (*Antilope cervicapra*)

The fawn hangs her head. She is being scolded by her mother yet again. So many do's and don'ts. So many rules to remember. Stay with the herd. ALL THE TIME!

Meanwhile, there's a whole wide world out there, waiting to be explored. Why doesn't her mother get that? What's the harm in wandering off for a bit and then returning after seeing some new sights?

Her mother keeps warning her about the big monsters that will chase you and bite your neck till you bleed and die, and then eat you up. Where are these big monsters? She hasn't seen any since she was born!

As she pretends to nibble at a patch of sweet grass, she makes up her mind. She will run away from the herd when the time is right. She will escape this life of restrictions and rules and go out there and explore the world to her heart's *content. Yes! That's what she will do. And no one, and nothing will ever stop her!*

It's five pm. Time for the last feed of the day. I take the measured scoop of milk powder, add it to the warm water, shake the bottle well to ensure it is all mixed up, then squeeze out a drop on the back of my hand to check the temperature. It's perfect, and when I make my way to my latest patient, she is waiting eagerly for her feed.

"Slow down, girl," I murmur, as I watch her greedily gulping the milk down.

This little fawn was brought to our centre a few days ago. She must have been just a few days old because remnants of her umbilical cord were still attached to her, rotting away.

Either she had wandered away from her mother, or she was an orphan.

She was dazed and skittish and tired. An initial examination had not revealed anything major – there were no wounds or injuries, and there was no internal damage. My task was to simply nurture her till she was ready to go back to the wild. Simpler said than done, for there were many challenges.

Her diet would initially be only milk because as a baby, she would have kept suckling her mother's udder as and when she wanted, and would not have begun eating grass as yet. We could not give her any animal milk for that could result in serious gut issues. So it was powdered milk only, prepared just like we would for a human baby. The fawn loved her milk, and waited impatiently for each of her five feeds. They were scheduled at six am, ten am, twelve pm, three pm, and five pm, and we had to be prompt, else she would get very worked up!

Deer are herbivores, meaning they eat only plants, including grass, fruits, leaves, vegetables, roots, etc. They have a very different digestive system, with multiple stomach chambers. Since plants have cellulose which is a difficult substance to digest, what happens is that when the deer first eats a plant, it uses its teeth to grind it down to small bits and the food goes to the first stomach chamber. Here it is softened and broken down further by special gut bacteria.

Then, the food is regurgitated – that is, it is sent back to the mouth. The deer then rechews the food, which is called cud now, and sends it to the next stomach chamber. Ruminants will chew the cud till the particle size of the food becomes very small, and then it is swallowed for bacterial and protazoal (microbial) digestion to start. Then the nutrients are finally absorbed by the deer's body, and waste excreted out in the form of pellets.

This type of digestion is very common to most herbivores, who are called ruminants. In fact, when you are thinking over a problem for a long time, it is said that you are ruminating over the issue. Ruminants will keep chewing the cud, or the regurgitated food, till it is completely digested.

Let me explain a little more about the rumination process so that our approach makes more sense.

At first, grass and plant material are quickly eaten and stored in the *rumen*, which is the first chamber.

When in a safe space and at peace, the animal will regurgitate small portions of ball-like grass into its mouth, masticate or chew it further into smaller particles and swallow into the rumen again, where fermentation takes place with the help of protozoa and other microbes to release energy in form of volatile fatty acids (not glucose) from plant matter like cellulose.

The second chamber is the *reticulum,* and the third chamber is the *omasum.* These two chambers handle more of the absorption of nutrients produced during the rumination, as well as water. The fourth chamber is the *abomasum.* This is a true stomach just like we have, where digestion of the milk happens.

So in infant herbivores, the first three chambers are present but have not yet started working, so the milk they feed on from the mother bypasses all the first three chambers going directly to the abomasum for digestion with enzymes, like humans. So to start the working of the complex first three chambers, grasses and plant matter have to be introduced gradually. The parents provide the rumen microbes with licking and other contact. If weaning is done too hastily, it can lead to severe bloating and death.

So it is extremely important for our little fawn to develop her gut properly. We can't be feeding her with just fruits and vegetables. In fact, keeping her on a diet of fruits could easily lead to bloating of her stomach and gas issues. We need to feed her a good mix of what she would normally eat in the jungle. We also need to introduce solids gradually, so that she gets used to the chewing and digestive processes.

After the first month of milk feeding, little teeth begin to show in the front of her mouth. Milk will no longer be sufficient, so we start including some long cut vegetables such as carrot, beetroot, beans, and cucumber in her diet. We also feed her grasses that mimic the forest vegetation. As we increase the plant content, we reduce the milk feeds so that it works just as a comfort feed whenever she needs it. At the same time, we begin to reduce contact and affection to make her used to becoming more aloof and shyer of people, which is essential if she needs to go into the wild.

Our fast-growing fawn is quickly outgrowing her sky kennel with a heating pad that she has been housed in till now. We shift her into an enclosure which has a mesh on top to prevent predators like leopards, civet cats, and mongoose that visit the centre often from climbing in and killing her. The enclosure also has a rough floor. This is to ensure that her hooves have the proper grip on the ground, else they might splay and she might fall, which would surely result in orthopaedic issues. We also need to give her calcium and multivitamin supplements that she would have normally obtained in the forest by licking mud beds that are rich with salts and vitamins.

We've now nicknamed her Bucky, for she is indeed a blackbuck (also called Krishna Mriga in Kannada). Note that blackbucks are completely different from deer. Spotted deer, which is deer, has horns that are shed every rutting season. Blackbucks are not deer, they are antelope, and their antlers are never shed, but keep growing through life. Blackbucks display sexual dimorphism which, to put it very simply, means that the two sexes exhibit different characteristics. Male blackbucks have spiral antlers and are dark chocolate brown in colour, whereas females have no antlers and are light brown and white in colour.

Bucky is extremely affectionate, often nuzzling my abdomen, and following me around the centre. I try to discourage her from being so friendly, for that is never good for wild creatures, but she doesn't take the hint and accosts me at every turn.

She's grown wonderfully now over a year, and it is time to move her out of the centre. Bucky has begun to show signs of growing up and becoming wiser. She appears to be shyer and more scared and aloof, not rushing towards us any more whenever she spots us. I would ideally like her to be released into the jungle, but she is not exactly ready for the wild and all that it brings. So it is deemed better for her to be moved to the zoo.

I dread the move, for it will be highly stressful for her. We would need to work quickly, handle her with gloves, possibly cover her head with a cloth so that she is not overly stimulated, and then bundle her into a truck. The journey in the truck, brief as it might be, will still be quite stressful. Then we need to move her again out of the truck and into the company of a herd of deer that are quite alien to her.

All this will increase her stress levels so high that she might just have a heart attack. Even if the move is successful and goes without a hitch, cortisol levels could remain high after everything, and result in her collapsing after some time. I really don't want her to be moved to the zoo, but there are no alternatives, so I accept the inevitable and proceed on making the appropriate arrangements.

In the meanwhile, we have had another wild deer added to our menagerie. We house the new deer with Bucky, hoping that the company will make her more comfortable, and make her transition to the zoo easier.

However, we are in for a major surprise!

One morning, my boy comes running to me just as I reach the centre.

"Akka! Akka! Bucky..." he pants.

"What happened? What happened to Bucky?" My heart begins to pound as I hurry behind him to the enclosure which houses the deer.

Let me describe the enclosure. It is round, with a concrete wall around four feet high on the circumference. There is a heavy wire netting that caps the wall. When we reach the enclosure, I stop short in shock.

Bucky has disappeared!

How on earth could this happen? The concrete wall ensures that Bucky could not have pushed through it. The heavy wire netting does not have any large gaps or anything that she could have squeezed through. But what really astounds me is that the heavy wire netting cap has actually been torn apart! There is no way that Bucky would have ripped it apart – it's impossible.

How did this happen at all? It's a complete mystery and quite baffles us all.

In a way, I am glad that Bucky got out of the move to the zoo. But at the same time, I am worried sick that something major has happened to her. The good thing is that there does not appear to be any blood or anything to indicate she was attacked. Leopards, wild dogs, and other predators can sometimes venture near our centre, but it does not look like this was the case.

We examine the area around the enclosure for clues, and sure enough, we find the vegetation around quite trampled, as if an elephant has travelled through it. We also find a few strands of the grasses we used to leave for Bucky as food.

The only plausible explanation we can come up with is that a wild elephant wandered here and saw the fresh grass we left for Bucky. The weather has been unseasonably hot of late, the forest is all dried up, which is probably why the elephant was wandering so far away from its usual route. The fresh green grass must have looked really tempting, and so the elephant had tried to get at it, destroying the enclosure in the process. Bucky and her companion must have slipped out after this, and wandered off into the forest.

We can't do much right now, except follow due process and report Bucky's escape. I often wonder how she is faring in the wild. Has she survived or fallen prey?

A couple of months later, one of my boys swears he saw Bucky and her companion disappearing into the forest with a herd of deer during the early morning hours. Of course we cannot confirm it, but I fondly hope that she is living her full life out there in the jungle, doing what she was born to do.

About the animal

- The Blackbuck (Antilope cervicapra) also called Indian Antelope, is found India and Nepal.

- It is active during the daytime, and can run at speeds of up to 80 kms per hour.

- It is a herbivore and also needs water daily.

- Males are heavier and darker than the females.

- Fun-fact: Cheetahs were used to hunt blackbucks since they are the only predator the antelope cannot outrun.

- The horns of the adult male are V-shaped, twisted spirally, and covered with deep ridges almost to the very top. The record length is 71.5cms!

<u>Why is it in danger?</u>

- The Blackbuck is one of the animals protected under the Indian Wildlife Act of 1972, under Schedule 1.

- Herds of blackbuck once roamed the Indian subcontinent extensively, but during the 20th century, they were hunted down and killed for sport so much that they almost became extinct.

- It is also in danger because of extensive deforestation, which leads to a loss of habitat.

11. TIPPING THE SCALES

Indian Pangolin (*Manis crassicaudata*)

The little baby pangolin clings on to its mother's tail as she ambles towards an anthill. Its scales are still soft, though beginning to harden quickly, and pale in colour. The mother sniffs around, then pauses in alarm. A moment later, she grabs her baby and coils around it firmly. She lays there motionless, half hidden in the sparse grass. She could easily be mistaken for a rock. Unfortunately, she's not so lucky.

A few minutes later, a couple of men approach, carrying a small bag. They pad softly towards the anthill.

"There!" One of the men whispers to the other, pointing to the lump on the ground.

The other man wraps a thick towel around his hand, drops to the floor, and grabs the coiled pangolin. He places it carefully in the bag and ties a knot at the top.

The two men grin at each other and trudge away. Their hunt has just begun.

The curled-up ball on the table poses a real problem. It's been half an hour and the ball lies as motionless as a rock. I take in a deep breath, trying to control my frustration.

Just then, a tiny head suddenly peeps out of the innermost coil, and I gasp. A few minutes later, a curious little baby pangolin crawls out, trying to figure out what is going on. The mother, however, does not care that her baby has escaped its safe house. She does not move a muscle. How on earth will I ever get around to examining her?

If you have never tried to uncoil a pangolin, I strongly suggest you do not attempt it. The sheer amount of pressure that the pangolin can resist is simply mind-boggling.

Pangolins, or scaly anteaters, have only this defence mechanism against their predators, and what an effective method it is!

This pangolin mom and her baby have been brought in today, and I need to evaluate her condition and propose a plan of action.

Pangolins are *myrmecophagous*. Isn't that a very impressive word? It simply means that pangolins are specialised for feeding on ants and termites. They have interesting features, specially evolved for this feeding habit. Can you imagine having a tongue as long as half your body? That's right – pangolins have really long tongues which are also very muscular and sticky. Perfect for dipping deep into an anthill and lapping up those delicious ants and termites! Pangolins possess a really strong sense of smell, and are able to detect their meal of insects using this sense. Though they primarily feed on ants and termites, they can also eat flies, worms, and crickets on the side. Interestingly, they also eat sand, stones and clay to aid in digestion. They have no teeth, but really strong stomach muscles. This makes them really difficult to hold captive, since serving up dishes of ants regularly is a bit tricky.

It also doesn't help that they are notoriously shy. Even the slightest hint of a threat will make them curl up into a tight ball and just lie there like a stone. Their scales are really hard and overlapping, making for a really good armour. Any predator who tries to bite will only injure its mouth.

Unfortunately, this makes them easy for poachers to pick up. Though pangolins are really difficult to spot, poachers are experts in animal behaviour and can predict where they can find their potential victims. Pangolins are poached for their scales, which are supposed to have immense medicinal value in traditional medicine, especially in China. Since the pangolin population has more or less been decimated there, poaching in neighbouring countries has picked up. It is ironic, since pangolin scales are just made of keratin, which is what human hair is made of! For every kilo of scales, almost double the number of pangolins is killed, which is tragic.

Pangolin meat is also considered to be a delicacy in some areas. After descaling, an average pangolin weighing around eight to ten kgs will yield just under a couple of kilos. So, a lot of pangolins need to be butchered in order to yield a reasonable amount of meat.

Pangolins are extremely essential to the ecosystem. As specialist eaters of ants and termites, they contribute to pest control in a huge way. Imagine if the forest was overrun by ants and termites! All the trees would become hollow in no time as the termites feast upon on the wood unchecked. By poaching pangolins, the delicate ecosystem of the wild is completely disrupted, and the repercussions promise to have a cascade effect. You might be surprised to know that pangolins are poached on a scale far greater than even the elephant and the tiger.

Coming back to my shy guest and her baby, I am able to do just a basic check. Her scales seem in good shape, showing a healthy pink tinge underneath. There do not seem to be any ticks or other parasites crawling around. She does not have any visible wounds or cuts either. If she were not in good health, she would not have such good control over her muscles and coil up so firmly. She would be more sluggish and open to my handling. All this points to no major issues. My best course of action appears to be to leave her undisturbed, so that she makes a full recovery on her own, without the additional stress of human intervention.

We house her in an enclosure and leave the tarpaulin on it. I would like to release her as soon as possible because it is difficult to feed her adequately in captivity. Hunting her protein-rich diet of ants and termites is something she is skilled at, and the sooner she can feed herself and her baby the right type of food, the better.

Extending her stay at the centre is putting not only her at risk, with increased exposure to domestic strains of bacteria and viruses, but also putting us humans at risk, since we too are exposed to unknown infections the wild animals might carry. In fact, right after releasing our pangolin, I came upon a study that showed pangolins carrying strains very similar to the Coronavirus, which as we all know caused such a deadly global pandemic. This is why I always advise folks not to be too adventurous and try and pet or fondle wild animals.

We leave her undisturbed. My boys report some nocturnal activity. The enclosure has a cement floor, for pangolins possess really strong claws and are expert burrowers. They dig with their strong forelimbs and claws, and use their hindlimbs and tail for support. So, an enclosure with a mud floor is not sufficient to hold the pangolin, for she can always dig her way out.

I am keen to release her as soon as possible, so in a week's time, she is taken out to the jungle along with her curious baby, who often crawls out of her coils and explores the world around it. Our lady has assumed her protective coiled shape again, and the boys leave her in the middle of the jungle. We wait for half an hour but she does not uncoil at all. She can probably still smell us. We move further away and return after some time, to an empty scene! She has disappeared, and so has her baby.

Another rescue and rehabilitation done and dusted. This is extremely special to me, because the last pangolin that was brought to our centre was badly injured and did not survive. That made me determined to ensure that my new guest was released safe and sound. That I could accomplish that with minimum stress to the pangolin and its baby really made my

day.

<u>About the animal</u>

- The Indian Pangolin (Manis crassicaudata) is native to the Indian subcontinent.

- It is found primarily in barren, hilly areas, though it can be found in grasslands and forests too, where an abundance of ants and termites can be found.

- It is nocturnal (active during the night).

- It digs and lives in burrows.

- Fun-fact: some of its burrows are large enough to even fit a human being

- So little is known about this shy creature that its lifespan in the wild is not known, though in captivity, it can live up to twenty years.

Why is it in danger?

- The Indian Pangolin is one of the animals protected under the Indian Wildlife Act of 1972, under Schedule 1.

- It is poached for its scales, which is used for medicinal purposes.

- Its meat is considered a delicacy.

- Its skin is also used for making bags, etc.

- Its habitat is threatened by rapid expansion of human development.

12. KISSING A COBRA

Spectacled Cobra (*Naja naja*)

It is getting hotter and hotter as the sun climbs the sky, and the earth lies parched and cracked below. The ground is like a blistering furnace, and anything that can breathe is hiding away in the shade. The city holds its breath while it bakes, a far cry from its past when it was once cool and pleasant.

The snake slithers across the paved surfaces, searching for a place to curl up and cool down. The soaring temperature is making it disoriented and it barely knows where it is going.

At last it finds an opening in the ground, and as it slides in, the coolness of the enclosed space underground is like a balm. It makes its way to the farthest corner and winds itself into a tight spiral, burrowing itself into the cold concrete as its body heat slowly dissipates.

Bliss, it thinks, little aware that danger lurks just above the surface.

The Spectacled Cobra holds a unique place in India. It is revered and worshipped, and many are the myths and stories we hear regarding it. At the same time, it is feared by everyone, and they are terrified, for good reason, of this particular snake.

The Spectacled Cobra (or Naagara Haavu in Kannada) is well-known for displaying the spectacled mark when it spreads its hood. Many Indian movies capitalize on this awe-inspiring sight and weave engrossing and quite unbelievable tales of love and revenge.

The cobra is a highly venomous snake, and if it bites a person, the muscles get paralyzed which could lead to respiratory failure or cardiac arrest. It is definitely not a creature to be trifled with, and people are well within reason to be scared of them.

However, the cobra that lies before me today is in such a pathetic state that it inspires sympathy in me, not fear.

"Is it dead, Akka?" The rescuer whispers, looking mournful. "Was I too late?"

I give a slight shake of my head, but I don't want to give him too much hope either.

"Let's first check everything," I say and he nods in agreement. As I begin my usual procedure of evaluation, the rescuer fills me in on what exactly happened.

As development in Bangalore spreads, encroachment on areas that were previously the domain of wild animals is normal. News of elephants and leopards straying into new areas of habitation is getting increasingly common. Snakes too are no exception.

This particular cobra was found curled up in an empty sump. The weather had become increasingly hot of late, and since snakes are cold-blooded, they need to regulate their body temperature based on their environment. This fellow was probably looking for a really cool place to beat the heat, and what better place than an empty sump that is sunk underground, and hence protected from the flaming heat outside?

If he had not been spotted, perhaps he would have just slithered away once it was dusk. Unfortunately for him, he was discovered, and as could be expected, all hell broke loose. It wasn't exactly clear what the folks who spotted him intended to do, but it did look like they were planning to burn him up. Otherwise, dousing him extensively with paint thinner didn't seem to have a point to scaring him away, did it? Sluggish to react when roused from his nap, the cobra did not escape the concentrated shower of paint thinner.

If you've ever sniffed at petrol or kerosene, you know how distinctive the smell is. Sniff too much of this or smell it for too long, and you will begin to feel nauseous. That is the nature of these fluids which contain certain toxic hydrocarbons, which can cause poisoning if ingested or inhaled for too long. This goes for paint thinners too.

In the case of the cobra, there are some other factors that are increasing the toxicity of the fumes. For one, snakes have a three-chambered heart, so there is a degree of inefficiency in the way their blood gets cleared of carbon-dioxide and enriched with oxygen during respiration. Secondly, the fumes have an aerosol effect, so they can actually penetrate the bloodstream. Thirdly, since snakes use their tongues to literally "taste" their environment, absorption of the fumes is much more than if it were just by inhalation. Last but not the least, the cooling of the body when the cobra went to sleep underground made him sluggish and reduced his metabolic activity.

The paint thinner fumes that emanate from the cobra are overwhelming, and I almost gag. He lies motionless and I can barely even sense a heartbeat. His body temperature is dipping and there does not appear to be any respiration going on at all.

I need to act fast if he is to have any chance of surviving at all. But this is the first time I've faced such a case, so what do I do? Thoughts are scrambling around my head, and I really need to pull myself together to think of any and all measures that might help.

Okay, I tell myself, this is a case of poisoning due to inhalation of paint thinner fumes. The cobra has inhaled all these paint thinner fumes, and it is shutting down everything because of respiratory paralysis. So the treatment has to be to increase the temperature, and start CPR to jumpstart the fading respiration and shallow heartbeat.

I use an infrared lamp for increasing the body temperature.

To get his heart going again, I can massage his heart gently and hope that helps to restore his beat. I show the rescuer how to massage the heart delicately, and he is all too glad to help.

How do I get normal respiration going though? I know what I need to do, but can I actually risk doing it to this highly venomous snake? I brush my doubts aside. I cannot – I will not just leave the cobra to die under my care, so I will do whatever is needed. Isn't that why I chose this profession?

I choose a little glass tube and place it between my mouth and the cobra's mouth. This is a flimsy barrier, definitely not something that will protect me if the cobra should suddenly revive and strike out. However, I am not worried, for the reptile shows absolutely no movement whatsoever. I begin to blow air into the cobra's nostrils and mouth.

The science behind this is very simple. When I breathe out, I am breathing out carbon-dioxide. This is what is entering the snake's nostrils. This gas will displace any paint thinner fumes that are circulating. And since the natural response of the respiratory system is to throw out carbon-dioxide, it will kick in, and as a result will draw in fresh oxygen. This is exactly what is needed to clear the system of the hazardous fumes.

"Akka is kissing a cobra!"

My boys are chuckling, both amused and somewhat awed, as they crowd outside the room, quite taken in by the bizarre sight. I dismiss them with a grin, and concentrate on blowing air into the cobra.

The rescuer and I take turns at blowing air and massaging the heart. We continue this for almost half an hour without a break, and are finally rewarded with a faint movement of the tail. The heartbeat too seems to be a little stronger. We need to wrap up things fast before the cobra becomes completely conscious.

I inject it with the required fluids and medicines, and we transfer it to a snake box which is completely covered, and is heated with a heat lamp. Now all we can do is to wait and watch.

Within an hour, the transformation is nothing short of miraculous.

Even though the cobra is still a bit sluggish in its movements, he is showing an almost complete recovery. He is able to follow movements of the finger, he is aggressive and he shows hooding.

Hooding is a defence mechanism adopted by the cobra. When confronted by a possible threat, it elongates its neck and spreads its neck muscles, which is called hooding. This is what displays the spectacled or rare monocled pattern that is unique in each cobra, which looks like ferocious eyes to the threat. By this menacing show, the cobra is effectively warning the intruder that if the latter ventures any closer, the cobra will not be held responsible for striking out and possibly killing it. Normally, intruders play better safe than sorry and flee.

Venom is a very precious commodity for the snake to manufacture, so it will never waste even a gram of venom on all the threats it comes across, but will use it very judiciously instead. Adult snakes have control over their venom glands and based on the size of prey, they will inject an exact amount of venom to digest that size of prey. So sometimes when confronted with humans who have inadvertently disturbed or stepped on the snake, they will bite, but not inject venom into the person (also called envenomation). They do this since they know that they are not going to eat the human, but are just angry for being disturbed. This is a called a *dry bite*. This bite will have teeth marks, blood, and pain too. In a *wet bite*, the venom too is injected. So it is quite difficult to distinguish immediately if the snake has inflicted a wet bite or a dry bite on the victim.

So if a person is ever bitten by a snake, they need to remain calm by telling themselves that it is a dry bite (even if it is a cobra bite), and promptly going to a proper hospital that stocks antivenom. This calmness will keep blood pressure from rising. If the blood pressure rises, complications increase.

Don'ts are:

- Don't panic

- Don't cut or suck point of bite

- Don't tied a torniquet/ or pressure bandage

Dos are:

- If possible, get a photo of snake, to ascertain if it is one of the four venomous snakes or not

- Remain calm

- Place splint on the bite area for support and immobilisation.

- Find closest hospital with antivenom and go there.

Since it is very difficult to distinguish between a wet and dry bite, the doctor will most probably start just a saline drip line, so that the vein is ready for administering the antivenom if symptoms begin to appear. Metrics such as body temperature, pulse, heart rate, and blood pressure, clotting and bleeding times will be monitored, apart from undergoing an ECG.

In half an hour or less, all these parameters will become erratic in a wet bite, which is when the antivenom will be administered intravenously in a saline drip slowly with constant monitoring.

In a dry bite, these parameters will return to normal soon, so just a saline drip, some pain killers and a tetanus injection is sufficient to go home. If antivenom is injected in a dry bite, since there is no venom in the system of the patient, this antivenom can cause kidney failure, anaphylactic shock and even death. So it is really important that antivenom is administered only in the case of a wet bit, and not otherwise.

Coming back to our dear cobra which has woken up in a strange environment, and is completely confused. He has no idea what has happened or if anything in this new environment contains any threat to him. Hence, he hoods aggressively, hoping that any threat in the vicinity will get the message and disappear.

For us, this is a very positive sign of healing, since the cobra is now able to respond to his environment and behave naturally.

I am thrilled and so is the rescuer.

"We did it!" We high-five each other, and laugh, all the tension melting away.

There is nothing more really for us to do, other than to procure the necessary permissions and release it into a deep part of the forest after forty-eight hours of observation.

I feel a sense of pride as I wrap up for the day. This was something I had never expected to encounter ever. Thinking out of the box and pulling out something that actually worked wonders and saved the cobra's life – that is incredible for me. Once again, I thank my stars that I never gave up, and just rolled up my sleeves and did whatever I could.

The famous verse from the Bhagvad Gita comes to my mind:

Karmanye vadhikaraste Ma Phaleshu Kadachana

Ma Karmaphalaheturbhurma Te Sangostvakarmani

Meaning:

You have the right to work only but never to its fruits.

Let not the fruits of action be your motive, nor let your attachment be to inaction.

Sometimes, that's all we can do.

About the animal

- The Spectacled Cobra (Naja naja) also called Indian Cobra, is found in the Indian subcontinent and its neighbouring countries, including Pakistan, Bangladesh, Sri Lanka, Nepal and Bhutan.

- It is found in a wide range of habitats, right from forests and grasslands to villages and cities.

- It can also vary a great deal in colours and patterns.

- It is oviparous and can lay between 10 and 30 eggs at a time.

- Fun-fact: It uses the movement of the snake charmer's pipe and the vibration of the ground to "dance", but is actually deaf and cannot hear the snake charmer's music.

- It is one of the "Big Four" snakes, which are responsible for the most number of human snakebites. The other three snakes are Russell's viper, Common krait, and Indian saw-scaled viper.

Why is it in danger?

- The Indian Cobra is one of the animals protected under the Indian Wildlife Act of 1972, under Schedule 2.

- It is often killed due to fear by humans.

- It is also often abused by snake charmers, and earlier, snake and mongoose fights were staged for money.

A Brief Note on The Wildlife Protection Act, 1972

What is it?

The Indian Parliament enacted this comprehensive Act in 1972, which gives all the details for safeguarding and protecting the wildlife flora and fauna in India.

Why is it needed?

India has an extremely rich and diverse ecosystem which needs to be preserved carefully. There are many species of flora and fauna that are native to India, and it must be ensured that they are protected at all costs.

How does the Act ensure protection?

- It gives the requirements for the formation of protected areas such as sanctuaries and national parks

- It gives details on how these areas should be governed, such as how advisory boards should be formed, what the powers and duties of wildlife wardens are, etc.

- It has a comprehensive list of the endangered wildlife in the country

- It has six schedules created to classify the wildlife and the kind of protection they will get

  - Schedule 1 and Schedule 2: endangered species with absolute protection and highest penalties for offences, no trading or hunting

  - Schedule 3 and Schedule 4: not endangered species with protection and lesser penalties for offences

o   Schedule 5: Animals that can be hunted

o   Schedule 6: Plants that are forbidden to be

cultivated

Some Useful Information

- For more information on the activities at WRRC, including how you can get involved, visit the website www.wrrcindia.org

- If you find any wild animal in distress, captivity, or being used for any illegal activities, you can contact us as follows:

  Email: communications@wrrcindia.org

  Phone: 8884023100 - Mr. Anand Nair

- In Bengaluru City, two other NGOs are involved in wildlife rescue and rehabilitation:

  ARRC - Phone number 9620286800

PFA – Phone number 9900025370 /

08028603986

- If you would like to contact either Dr. Roopa Satish

  or Anitha Murthy for any reason related to the

  book, please email <u>friendsoftripod@gmail.com</u>

Acknowledgments

I would like to thank all the trustees of WRRC Ms. Suparna Ganguly, Dr Sheila Rao, Ms. Brindha Nandakumar, Ms. Sandhya Madappa, Mr. Gopi Shankar, Ms. Shalini Santosh, and Mr. Subrahmanian Santakumar, for their commitment and dedication to wildlife rescue and rehabilitation.

I am grateful to Mr. Anand Nair, Supervisor, Bannerghatta rehabilitation centre, WRRC for the amazing work he has been doing for past 20 years in wildlife rehabilitation. His passion, dedication, and practical approach to solve any situation is truly a gift.

I would not be able to do the work I do if not for my boys at the centre who are so brave, cautious, yet kind and gentle as they restrain the scared, angry, and stressed-out wildlife coming to the centre. Mr. Girimada, Dharma, Kiran, and Manoj are the back bone of our work.

I would like to thank the office staff of WRRC for supporting us in backend functions.

I would like to thank all the personnel of BBMP forest cell, independent rescuers, volunteers, and the kind public who rescue the injured wildlife. I am thankful to all the generous donors of WRRC for supporting us in this endeavour.

I would like to thank Dr Sunil Panwar, Executive director, Bengaluru Bannerghatta Biological park, and Mr Prabhakar Prasiddha, DFO, Bannerghatta National park, and all the forest department staff who are working tirelessly for the upkeep and maintenance of our wild areas and wildlife.

Dr. Roopa Satish

When I met Dr. Roopa, I was blown away not just by her work, but by her passion and deep beliefs about life itself. I was immediately itching to write something with her, and she had thoughts of this too. This book was born out of our collaboration. I am deeply indebted to her for permitting me to engage with her and have a hand in narrating her adventures, which are no doubt exciting, but also, in some cases, life-threatening. That she is able to calmly recount these stories and even laugh about them bears testament to the strength of her character. For someone who has a fear of all animals, this is the best I can experience in terms of close encounters of the wildlife kind. It has been a wonderful, educative journey, and I sincerely hope this book finds the wide, curious, and compassionate audience it deserves. Thank you, Dr. Roopa!

I would also like to thank the Writeous Women – Fehmida Zakeer, Jyoti Vinod, Shruthi Rao, and Vrinda Baliga, who were so encouraging, supportive, and always ready to help.

Special thanks to Vrinda, who has done so much hand-holding for my foray into self-publishing, and upon whom I have relied extensively, to bring this book thus far.

Anitha Murthy